SWEDEN TRAVE[...]
BOOK 2023 AND [...]

An In-Depth Guide to Sweden: [...]overing Hidden
Gems, Where to Stay, What to Do, Itineraries, Maps
and Directions, and much more

Kian Wright

DISCLAIMER

This book is a work of fiction. Names, characters, places, and incidents either are the product of the author's imagination or are used fictitiously. Any resemblance to actual persons, living or dead, events, or locales is entirely coincidental.

Copyright © 2023 by Kian Wright

All rights reserved. No part of this book may be reproduced, scanned, or distributed in any printed or electronic form without permission. Please do not participate in or encourage piracy of copyrighted materials in violation of the author's rights. Purchase only authorized editions.

This book is licensed for your enjoyment only. It may not be re-sold or given away to other people. If you would like to share this book with another person, please purchase an additional copy for each recipient. If you're reading this book and did not purchase it, or it was not purchased for your use only, then please return it to your favourite bookseller and purchase your copy. Thank you for respecting the hard work of this author.

This book is published by Kian Wright, and all rights are reserved by the publisher.

Disclaimer

The information contained in this book is for general information purposes only.

The information is provided by the author and while we endeavour to keep the information up to date and correct, we make no representations or warranties of any kind, express or implied, about the completeness, accuracy, reliability, suitability, or availability concerning the book or the information, products, services, or related graphics contained in the book for any purpose. Any reliance you place on such information is therefore strictly at your own risk. In no event will the author or publisher be liable for any loss or damage including without limitation, indirect or consequential loss or damage, or any loss or damage whatsoever arising from loss of data or profits arising out of, or in connection with, the use of this Book. Please note that this disclaimer is subject to change without notice.

TABLE OF CONTENT

Introduction to Sweden

Welcome to Sweden, a captivating Scandinavian country known for its picturesque landscapes, rich history, and warm hospitality. Whether you're a seasoned traveller, an adventurous soul, or a curious tourist, Sweden offers a myriad of experiences that are sure to leave you enchanted. So, fasten your seatbelts and let's embark on an unforgettable journey through this stunning Nordic nation.

Geography and Climate:

Sweden, located in Northern Europe, shares borders with Norway and Finland. Its diverse geography encompasses dense forests, majestic mountains, and thousands of picturesque islands dotting the Baltic Sea. The country experiences four distinct seasons, with mild summers and cold winters. Be sure to pack appropriate clothing and prepare for the possibility of witnessing the magical Northern Lights during winter.

Cultural Delights:

Swedish culture is a harmonious blend of ancient traditions and modern influences. Embrace the concept of "lagom" (the art of balance) as you immerse yourself in the Swedish lifestyle. Discover the vibrant arts scene in Stockholm, the capital city, and explore world-class museums like the Vasa Museum and ABBA Museum. Indulge in fika, a beloved Swedish tradition of taking a break for coffee and pastries. Try traditional dishes like meatballs, gravlax (cured salmon), and cinnamon buns (kanelbullar) to tantalize your taste buds.

Majestic Cities and Charming Towns:

Start your Swedish adventure in Stockholm, often called the "Venice of the North." Stroll through the Gamla Stan (Old Town) with its narrow cobblestone streets and colourful buildings. Explore the Royal Palace and witness the Changing of the Guard. Don't miss the chance to visit Gothenburg, a vibrant coastal city known for its picturesque canals, trendy boutiques, and world-class seafood.

Venture further north to Kiruna, where you can experience the mesmerizing Icehotel, constructed entirely of ice and snow. Take a leisurely walk through Malmö, a charming city with a modern twist, and cross the iconic Øresund Bridge to explore Copenhagen, Denmark's capital.

For a glimpse into traditional Swedish life, visit the idyllic towns of Ystad, Uppsala, and Visby. These historic gems offer well-preserved architecture, cobblestone streets, and a glimpse into the nation's past.

Nature's Wonderland:

Sweden's unspoiled natural beauty is a treasure trove for outdoor enthusiasts. Explore the stunning archipelagos of Stockholm, where you can sail, kayak, or swim in crystal-clear waters. Embark on a hiking adventure through the awe-inspiring landscapes of Abisko National Park or Sarek National Park, known for its pristine wilderness and Arctic wildlife.

Head to the Swedish Lapland for a once-in-a-lifetime experience. Discover the indigenous Sami culture, go dog sledging or snowmobiling, and even stay in an ice hotel. The magical Midnight Sun during summer and the chance to witness the dancing Northern Lights in winter make this region truly extraordinary.

Festivals and Traditions:

Sweden hosts a variety of vibrant festivals and celebrations throughout the year. Join the Midsummer festivities in June, where locals gather to dance around maypoles, feast on herring, and embrace the long summer days. Experience the joyous Lucia celebrations in December, marked by candlelit processions and traditional music.

Practical Information:

Sweden has a well-developed infrastructure and an efficient public transportation system. English is widely spoken, making it easy to communicate with locals. Remember to carry Swedish Krona (SEK) for cash transactions, although credit and debit cards are widely accepted.

Sustainability and Outdoor Etiquette:

Sweden is at the forefront of sustainable living and eco-tourism. Embrace the Swedish principle of "allemansrätt" (the freedom to roam) by respecting nature and practising outdoor etiquette. Leave no trace behind, and always follow designated trails and guidelines to preserve the pristine environment.

Safety and Security:

Sweden is known for its safety and security. However, it is always wise to take standard precautions such as keeping an eye on your belongings and being aware of your surroundings, especially in crowded areas or tourist hotspots.

Getting Around:

Sweden has an extensive transportation network, making it easy to navigate the country. The efficient train system connects major cities, while buses and ferries serve smaller towns and remote areas. Domestic flights are also available for longer distances. Consider purchasing the "Sweden Travel Pass" for unlimited travel on public transportation.

Unique Experiences:

Enhance your Swedish adventure with these unique experiences:

- Stay in a traditional red cottage (stuga) in the countryside and embrace the tranquillity of the Swedish countryside.
- Explore the Stockholm Archipelago by hopping on a boat tour or chartering your el.
- Take a sauna and indulge in the invigorating tradition of a cold dip in a nearby lake or the sea.
- Visit the Icehotel in Jukkasjärvi and sleep on a bed made of ice.
- Join a guided moose safari and encounter these majestic creatures in their natural habitat.
- Try ice fishing on a frozen lake during winter or experience the thrill of dog sledging.

Remember, this guide only scratches the surface of what Sweden has to offer. So, get ready to be captivated by

Sweden's stunning landscapes, embrace its unique traditions, and create memories that will last a lifetime. Enjoy your journey through this enchanting Scandinavian gem!

Planning Your Trip to Sweden

It might be thrilling to organise a trip to Sweden! Sweden has a variety of attractions, from bustling cities to breathtaking natural scenery. You can use the following procedures to organise your vacation to Sweden:

Sweden at a Glance:

- Northern Europe is the home of Sweden, sometimes referred to as the Kingdom of Sweden.
- The nation is renowned for its stunning natural scenery, which includes mountains, lakes, and forests.

- Sweden is well known for its cutting-edge technology, fashion, and design.
- The official language is Swedish, and around 10 million people are living there.
- The Swedish Krona (SEK) is the official currency.

Ideal Season to Visit:
- The summer season (June to August) is perfect for outdoor activities, festivals, and city exploration due to the nice weather and extended daylight hours.
- Winter (December to February) is the best time to participate in winter sports like skiing and ice skating and to see the enchanted Northern Lights in Swedish Lapland.
- The months of spring (March to May) and fall (September to November) provide cooler temperatures, stunning foliage and fewer tourists.

How to Get There:
- **By Air:** Stockholm Arlanda Airport is Sweden's main international airport and has good connections to major cities all over the globe.
- **By railway:** Using attractive routes across gorgeous landscapes, the railway network links Sweden to its neighbours, notably Denmark, Norway, and Finland.
- **By Ferry:** You may choose to go to Sweden by ferry from Finland or Denmark while taking in the breathtaking archipelagos along the route.

Must-Visit Destinations:
Stockholm:
- The biggest capital of Sweden is referred to as the "Venice of the North."
- Check out the Royal Palace and the quaint Old Town (Gamla Stan), which has cobblestone streets and colourful houses.

- Visit renowned museums including the Fotografiska, ABBA: The Museum, and the Vasa Museum.

Gothenburg:
- The second-largest city in Sweden is renowned for its dynamic environment and thriving culinary scene.
- Visit the Universeum, an interactive science museum, or stroll along the Liseberg amusement park's gorgeous canals.
- The Gothenburg Archipelago, which has breathtaking scenery and quaint fishing communities, should not be missed.

Malmö:
- Located in southern Sweden, on the other side of the bridge from Copenhagen, the capital of Denmark.
- Visit the renowned Turning Torso skyscraper and explore the Western Harbor's (Västra Hamnen) contemporary architecture.
- Explore Malmö Castle, the city's historical core, and enjoy a stroll in Kungsparken.

Swedish Lapland:
- Visit Sweden's Arctic area for a very unique experience.
- For a chance to view the captivating Northern Lights, go to Kiruna (best seen between September and March).
- Engage in exhilarating winter sports like dog sledging asledgingobiling while exploring the Icehotel in Jukkasjärvi, a hotel built of ice and snow.

Gotland:
- The biggest island in Sweden is renowned for its gorgeous scenery and mediaeval buildings.

- Visit Visby, a quaint village with restored city walls and cobblestone streets that is a UNESCO World Heritage site.
- Explore historic ruins, relax on the island's lovely beaches, and take in the vibrant cultural scene.

Transportation Within Sweden:
- Sweden has a well-functioning public transit system that includes trains, buses, trams, and subways. The national railway company, SJ, provides relaxing train rides between major cities.
- Renting a vehicle is a fantastic alternative if you want more freedom or want to explore rural locations. Sweden's roads are kept in good condition, and driving is typically safe. Just keep in mind to familiarise yourself with any applicable local traffic laws.

Accommodation Options:
- **Hotels:** There are several hotels in Sweden, ranging in price from luxurious to affordable. International hotel companies and quaint boutique hotels are also available.
- **Hostels:** These are a terrific option if you're on a tight budget or like a more communal setting. They provide inexpensive lodging and a chance to interact with other travellers.
- **Guesthouses and Bed & Breakfasts:** These accommodations provide a cosier, more intimate environment, sometimes in old-fashioned Swedish homes or rural areas.
- **Vacation rentals:** You may have your own space and experience local life by renting an apartment, a cottage or a villa via Airbnb or another vacation rental company.

Currency and Money Matters:

- The Swedish Krona (SEK) is the country's official currency. For modest transactions, it's a good idea to have some local cash on hand, although credit and debit cards are accepted almost everywhere in the nation.
- Although there are many ATMs in cities and towns, it's a good idea to let your bank know about your vacation plans to prevent any problems with card use.
- In Sweden, gratuities are seldom expected since most invoices contain a service fee. However, for great service, rounding up the amount or adding a modest gratuity is appreciated.

Language and Communication:

- The majority of Swedes speak good English, particularly in tourist regions and bigger cities, even though Swedish is the country's official language. During your vacation, communication should not be a problem.

Local Customs and Etiquette:

- Sweden values privacy and personal space. Respect their limits and refrain from needless physical touch.
- Sweden's culture places a great priority on punctuality. To avoid missing appointments or excursions, be prompt.
- A handshake is the most typical way to greet someone when you first meet them. Be prepared to be addressed by your first name since Swedes often use them, especially in official settings.
- In Sweden, it is customary to take off your shoes before entering a house, so do what the host directs.

Outdoor Activities and Nature:

- Sweden is well known for having beautiful natural scenery. Utilise abundant alternatives for outdoor recreation.
- Hiking: Take to the trails and spectacular vistas of national parks including Abisko, Sarek, and Tyresta.
- Enjoy the magnificent lakes and rivers, especially the Stockholm Archipelago, which is made up of hundreds of islands, while canoeing and kayaking.
- Join a guided trip to see moose, reindeer, and other animals in their natural settings on a wildlife safari.
- Bicycle: With beautiful routes like Kattegattleden and the Göta Canal, Sweden has a developed bicycle infrastructure.

Safety and Health:
- Excellent medical facilities are available in Sweden, and emergency services may be obtained by dialling 112.
- As medical treatment in Sweden may be costly for travellers, it is advised to obtain travel insurance that covers medical costs.
- Generally speaking, Sweden is a secure nation, but it's always a good idea to take security measures, such as being alert to your surroundings and watching after your valuables.

COVID-19 Travel Recommendations:
- Before and throughout your journey to Sweden, keep yourself informed on the most recent COVID-19-related travel restrictions and requirements.
- Check to see whether you must arrive in quarantine or with confirmation of a negative test or immunisation.

- Follow all applicable rules and regulations for mask use, social distance, and other unique specifications for lodging, dining, and attractions in your area.

Dining and Cuisine:
- The cuisine in Sweden is exceptional. Don't pass up the opportunity to sample traditional Swedish fare like lingonberry jam, herring, gravlax (cured salmon), and meatballs (köttbullar).
- A popular Swedish custom known as fika involves stopping for coffee and a sweet treat. Enjoy delectable sweets like cardamom and cinnamon buns (kanelbullar and kardemummabullar, respectively).
- Find regional cafes and restaurants to enjoy real Swedish food. Organic and locally sourced foods are often used in restaurants.

Cultural Experiences:
- To learn about the history, culture, and folklore of Sweden, go to open-air museums like Skansen in Stockholm or the Old Town in Lule.
- If you're coming in late June, take part in a Midsommar celebration, which is a traditional Swedish holiday. It's a happy event with music, flower crowns, and local cuisine.
- Investigate the Swedish art and design scene. Visit modern Swedish art and design galleries, studios, and cutting-edge museums.

Shopping and Souvenirs:
- Sweden is well known for its fashion and design. Seek distinctive Scandinavian fabrics, pottery, glassware, and glass as mementoes.
- Visit regional markets to enjoy local specialities and buy fresh products, such as the Stermalm Food Hall

in Stockholm or the Haga neighbourhood in Gothenburg.

- In Sweden, candy is known as "godis," and there are many different sweets available to satiate your sweet tooth.

Sustainable Travel:

- Sweden is renowned for its dedication to environmental protection. Think about adopting environmentally friendly modes of transportation, such as public transit or renting bicycles.
- You may enjoy the countryside responsibly and protect the environment by adhering to the "allemansrätten" (the right of public access) principles.
- Consider staying at eco-certified hotels and supporting regional companies that place a high priority on sustainability.

Learn Some Swedish Phrases:

While many Swedes speak English, learning a few basic Swedish phrases can enhance your interactions and show appreciation for the local culture.

Here are a few essential phrases:

- Hej (Hey) - Hello
- Tack (Tahk) - Thank you
- Ursäkta (Ur-sheck-ta) - Excuse me
- Ja (Ya) - Yes
- Nej (Nay) - No
- Var är...? (Var air) - Where is...?
- Kan jag få men? (Kahn ya foh men-en) - Can I have the menu?

Planning your trip well in advance will ensure a smooth and enjoyable experience in Sweden. Embrace the unique blend of nature, culture, and design that this beautiful country has to offer.

Exploring Stockholm, the Capital City

Stockholm, the capital city of Sweden, is a beautiful and vibrant destination that offers a wide range of attractions and activities for travellers and tourists.

Here are some highlights and recommendations for exploring Stockholm:

Gamla Stan (Old Town):

Gamla Stan (Old Town)

Gamla Stan (Old Town)

Start your visit by exploring Gamla Stan, the historic heart of Stockholm. Wander through narrow cobblestone streets, admire the colourful buildings, and visit iconic attractions like the Royal Palace and Stockholm Cathedral. Don't forget to browse the charming shops and enjoy a fika (Swedish coffee break) at one of the local cafés.

Vasa Museum:

A must-visit for history buffs, the Vasa Museum is home to the Vasa warship, a 17th-century warship that sank on its maiden voyage and was salvaged in the 1960s. The museum showcases the well-preserved ship and provides insight into Sweden's maritime history.

Skansen Open-Air Museum:

Skansen Open-Air Museum

Located on Djurgården Island, Skansen is the world's oldest open-air museum. It features historic buildings from various parts of Sweden, including farms, windmills, and traditional houses. You can also observe Nordic wildlife at the adjacent zoo.

Djurgården Island:

Apart from Skansen, Djurgården offers a range of other attractions. Visit the ABBA Museum, dedicated to the famous Swedish band, or explore the Grona Lund amusement park for thrilling rides. Nature lovers can take a stroll through the lush green spaces or rent a bike to explore the island.

Stockholm Archipelago:

Take a boat tour or ferry to explore the Stockholm Archipelago, a vast network of over 30,000 islands, islets, and rocks. Enjoy the stunning natural scenery, go fishing, or visit one of the inhabited islands for a unique cultural experience.

Moderna Museet:

Art enthusiasts should head to the Moderna Museet, Stockholm's museum of modern and contemporary art. The museum features works by renowned artists like Picasso, Dalí, and Warhol, as well as a collection of Swedish art.

Drottningholm Palace:

Venture outside the city centre to visit the Drottningholm Palace, a UNESCO World Heritage site. This magnificent palace is the official residence of the Swedish royal family and is surrounded by beautiful gardens. Don't miss the chance to watch an opera or ballet performance at the Drottningholm Palace Theatre.

Food and Fika:

Stockholm offers a diverse culinary scene. Sample traditional Swedish dishes like meatballs, herring, and gravlax, or explore international cuisine in the trendy neighbourhoods of Södermalm and Östermalm. Don't forget to indulge in a fika, a Swedish tradition of taking a break with coffee and pastries.

Stockholm City Hall:

Visit the Stockholm City Hall, famous for hosting the Nobel Banquet each year. Take a guided tour to admire the magnificent halls and enjoy panoramic views of the city from the tower.

Shopping:

Stockholm is a shopping paradise, with options ranging from high-end fashion to vintage boutiques and design stores. Stroll along Drottninggatan, the city's main shopping street, or explore the upscale department stores NK and Åhléns.

Note: This is just brief as we will still dwell more on shopping as we continue on this guide.

The breakdown of directions, transportation options, prices, and availability for each of the mentioned places in Stockholm:

Gamla Stan (Old Town):

By foot: Gamla Stan is easily accessible on foot from the city centre.

Public transportation: You can also take the metro (T-bana) to Gamla Stan station (red and green lines).

Price: Walking is free, and the metro fare depends on the ticket type (single ticket: around 32 SEK).

Availability: Gamla Stan is open to visitors throughout the day, but individual shops and attractions may have varying opening hours.

Vasa Museum:

By foot/public transportation: From Gamla Stan, you can walk or take bus number 65 to the Vasa Museum.

Price: Bus fare depends on the ticket type (single ticket: around 32 SEK).

Availability: The Vasa Museum is open daily, with varying hours (check their website for the most up-to-date information).

Skansen Open-Air Museum:

Public transportation: Take tram number 7 or bus number 67 to the Skansen stop in Djurgården.

Price: Public transportation fare depends on the ticket type (single ticket: around 32 SEK).

Availability: Skansen is open year-round, but hours vary depending on the season (check their website for current opening hours).

Djurgården Island:

By foot/public transportation: You can reach Djurgården by walking from the city centre or taking bus number 69.

Price: Bus fare depends on the ticket type (single ticket: around 32 SEK).

Availability: Djurgården is open year-round, and attractions have varying opening hours (check individual websites for details).

Stockholm Archipelago:

By boat: Several companies offer boat tours from Stockholm to explore the archipelago. You can find options at Strömkajen or Nybrokajen.

Price: Boat tour prices vary depending on the provider and duration (around 200-500 SEK).

Availability: Boat tours are usually available during the summer season (May to September) but check with specific providers for schedules.

Moderna Museet:

By foot/public transportation: Moderna Museet is located on the island of Skeppsholmen, accessible by foot or bus number 65.

Price: Bus fare depends on the ticket type (single ticket: around 32 SEK).

Availability: Moderna Museet has varying opening hours, so check their website for the most up-to-date information.

Drottningholm Palace:

By car: Drottningholm Palace is about a 20-minute drive from the city centre.

Price: Parking fees may apply at Drottningholm Palace.

Availability: The palace and gardens are open for visitors, but check their website for specific opening hours and tour availability.

Food and Fika:

Restaurants and cafés are scattered throughout Stockholm, easily accessible by foot or public transportation.

Prices: Food and beverage prices vary depending on the establishment.

Availability: Opening hours of restaurants and cafés may vary, but you'll find options available throughout the day.

Stockholm City Hall:

By foot/public transportation: Stockholm City Hall is located in the city centre and easily reachable on foot or by bus/metro.

Price: Public transportation fare depends on the ticket type (single ticket: around 32 SEK).

Availability: Stockholm City Hall is open for guided tours, but check their website for tour schedules and availability

Shopping:

Shopping areas like Drottninggatan, Södermalm, and Östermalm are best explored on foot.

Public transportation: You can use the metro or buses to reach these areas.

Price: Public transportation fare depends on the ticket type (single ticket: around 32 SEK).

Availability: Most shops in Stockholm are open during regular business hours, but individual store hours may vary.

It's important to note that the prices mentioned for public transportation are approximate and subject to change. Stockholm has an efficient public transportation system, including buses, trams, and the metro (T-bana), which can be accessed using the same ticket.

For specific opening hours and tour availability of the attractions mentioned, it's always recommended to check the official websites below or contact the respective places directly. Opening hours and availability may vary depending on the season, holidays, and any special events.

Additionally, if you prefer to explore Stockholm by car, it's essential to consider parking availability and costs, especially in the city centre where parking can be limited and expensive. Public transportation is often a convenient and cost-effective option for getting around Stockholm.

Here is the contact information or contact address for each of the mentioned places in Stockholm:

Gamla Stan (Old Town):
Address: Gamla Stan, 111 29 Stockholm, Sweden
Website: https://www.visitstockholm.com/o/gamla-stan/
Contact: +46 8 508 285 08

Vasa Museum:
Address: Galärvarvsvägen 14, 115 21 Stockholm, Sweden
Website: https://www.vasamuseet.se/
Contact: +46 8 519 548 80

Skansen Open-Air Museum:
Address: Djurgårdsslätten 49-51, 115 21 Stockholm, Sweden
Website: www.skansen.se/
Contact: +46 8 442 8000

Djurgården Island:
Address: Djurgården, 115 21 Stockholm, Sweden

Stockholm Archipelago:
As the Stockholm Archipelago consists of numerous islands, it is recommended to contact specific tour operators for boat tours and island visits.

Moderna Museet:
Address: Exercisplan 4, 111 49 Stockholm, Sweden
Website: www.modernamuseet.se/stockholm/sn
Contact: +46 8 520 235 00

Drottningholm Palace:
Address: Drottningholms Slott Slottsstallet 11, 178 93 Drottningholm, Sweden
Website: https://www.kungligaslotten.se/vara-besoksmal/drottningholms-slott.html

Contact: +46 8 402 61 00

Food and Fika:

As there are numerous restaurants and cafés in Stockholm, it is recommended to explore the areas of interest and choose based on personal preference. Websites such as TripAdvisor or Yelp can provide reviews and contact information for specific establishments.

Stockholm City Hall:

Address: Hantverkargatan 1, 111 52 Stockholm, Sweden

Website: https://stadshuset.stockholm/

Contact: +46 8 508 290 00

Shopping:

Drottninggatan: Located in the city centre of Stockholm.

Sneighbourhoodneighborhood in Stockholm is known for its shopping streets such as Götgatan and Hornsgatan.

Östermalm: A district in Stockholm with high-end shopping areas such as Biblioteksgatan and Sturegallerian.

Discovering Gothenburg and the West Coast

Gothenburg

Gothenburg and the West Coast of Sweden are beautiful destinations for travellers and tourists alike. Whether you're interested in history, nature, or vibrant city life, this region offers a variety of attractions and activities to explore.

Here are some highlights to consider during your visit:
Gothenburg City:

Start your journey in Gothenburg, the second-largest city in Sweden. Wander along the picturesque canals of the Linné and Haga districts, lined with colourful houses, trendy cafes, and boutiques. Visit the Gothenburg Museum of Art, Universeum Science Center, and the iconic Liseberg amusement park. Don't forget to take a relaxing boat tour through the city's archipelago.

Gothenburg Archipelago:

Just off the coast of Gothenburg, you'll find a stunning archipelago with over 20 islands to explore. Take a ferry or boat tour to picturesque islands like Vrångö, Styrsö, or Brännö. Enjoy leisurely walks along the beaches, discover charming fishing villages, and indulge in delicious seafood at local restaurants.

Marstrand:

Located about an hour north of Gothenburg, Marstrand is a charming island known for its beautiful scenery and sailing culture. Explore the historical Carlstens Fortress, visit the quaint shops and cafes along the marina, and relax on the island's sandy beaches. Marstrand is also famous for hosting the annual Match Cup in Sweden, a prestigious sailing event.

Bohuslän Coast:

The Bohuslän Coast stretches along the western shoreline, offering stunning rocky landscapes and picturesque fishing villages. Don't miss the picturesque village of Smögen, known for its vibrant wooden houses and bustling harbour. Take a boat trip to the Koster Islands, a marine national park with unique flora and fauna, perfect for hiking and kayaking.

Tjörn and Orust Islands:

Orust Island

Tjörn Island

Tjörn and Orust are two larger islands in the archipelago, known for their scenic beauty and cultural attractions. Explore the Nordic Watercolor Museum on Tjörn, which combines art with nature, and visit the charming village of Skärhamn.In August, visit the picturesque fishing village of Mollösund and enjoy the pristine beaches and scenic hiking trails.

Fjällbacka:

Further up the coast, you'll find Fjällbacka, a charming coastal town famous for its connection to Swedish author Camilla Läckberg's crime novels. Explore the picturesque streets, visit Ingrid Bergman Square (honouring the renowned actress who had a summer house here), and climb up to Theteberget Rock for breathtaking views of the archipelago.

Liseberg and Gothenburg Culture:

Liseberg and Gothenburg entertainment night
If you're travelling with family or seeking entertainment, Liseberg amusement park is a must-visit. With thrilling rides, beautiful gardens, and lively entertainment, it offers fun for all ages. Additionally, Gothenburg has a vibrant cultural scene with numerous theatres, concert venues, and festivals throughout the year.
Seafood Delights:

The West Coast is renowned for its fresh seafood. Sample local delicacies like freshly caught shrimp, crayfish, lobster, and herring. Visit the Feskekôrka (Fish Church) in Gothenburg, a seafood market housed in a distinctive building, or indulge in a seafood buffet at one of the many restaurants along the coast.

This is a guide on how to get to each place mentioned, along with transportation options, availability, contact information, addresses, and approximate prices:

Gothenburg City:

By Car: Gothenburg has well-developed road networks, and you can reach the city by car via the E6 or E20 highways.

By Public Transportation: Gothenburg is served by an extensive public transportation system, including buses and trams. You can easily get around the city using public transportation.

Availability and Opening Hours: Public transportation operates throughout the day, with varying schedules. Most attractions in the city have their opening hours, so it's best to check their websites for specific details.

Contact Information: Västtrafik is the public transportation authority in Gothenburg. You can find information about routes, schedules, and tickets on their website (https://www.vasttrafik.se/)

Address: Gothenburg City Center.

Gothenburg Archipelago:

By Ferry: Several ferry operators offer transportation to different islands in the Gothenburg Archipelago, including Vrångö, Styrsö, and Brännö. Some popular ferry companies are Styrsöbolaget (https://www.styrsobolaget.se/) and Västtrafik (https://www.vasttrafik.se/)

Availability and Opening Hours: Ferry schedules vary depending on the season, but generally, there are regular departures throughout the day. It's recommended to check the ferry company's website for up-to-date schedules.

Contact Information: Styrsöbolaget can be reached at +46 31 65 07 50.

Address: Ferry terminals are located in Saltholmen, which is about a 30-minute tram ride from Gothenburg city centre.

Marstrand:

By Car: Marstrand is about an hour's drive north of Gothenburg. You can reach it via the E6 highway.

By Public Transportation: Take a bus from Gothenburg Central Station to Marstrand. Bus services are operated by Västtrafik.

Availability and Opening Hours: Buses to Marstrand run regularly, but it's recommended to contact them for updated schedules. Carlstens Fortress on Marstrand has specific opening hours.

Contact Information: Västtrafik can be reached at +46 771 41 43 00.

Address: Marstrand, Kungälv Municipality.

Bohuslän Coast:

By Car: The Bohuslän Coast is easily accessible by car. Highways E6 and E45 connect various towns and villages along the coast.

By Public Transportation: Public buses operated by Västtrafik connect different parts of the Bohuslän Coast. You can contact them for specific routes and schedules.

Availability and Opening Hours: Bus schedules vary.

Contact Information: Västtrafik can be reached at +46 771 41 43 00.

Address: Various towns and villages along the Bohuslän Coast.

Tjörn and Orust Islands:

By Car: Tjörn and Orust are connected to the mainland by bridges, making them easily accessible by car.

By Public Transportation: Public buses operated by Västtrafik serve Tjörn and Orust Islands. You can check the Västtrafik website for specific bus routes and schedules.

Availability and Opening Hours: Bus schedules vary depending on the route and season. It's advisable to contact them for the most up-to-date information on schedules. Opening hours for attractions, museums, and restaurants on the islands may vary, so it's best to contact them

Contact Information: Västtrafik can be reached at +46 771 41 43 00.

Address: Tjörn and Orust Islands are located in the Bohuslän region, west of Gothenburg. The exact addresses will vary depending on the specific location or attraction you plan to visit.

Fjällbacka:

By Car: Fjällbacka is approximately a 1.5-hour drive north of Gothenburg. You can reach it by following the E6 highway.

By Public Transportation: Take a train from Gothenburg Central Station to Uddevalla, and then transfer to a bus to Fjällbacka. Bus services are operated by Västtrafik.

Availability and Opening Hours: Train and bus schedules vary, so it's advisable to contact them for up-to-date information. Opening hours for attractions and restaurants in Fjällbacka may vary, so it's best to intact them dire.

Contact Information: Västtrafik can be reached at +46 771 41 43 00.

Address: Fjällbacka, Tanum Municipality.

Liseberg and Gothenburg Culture:

By Car: Liseberg amusement park and most cultural attractions in Gothenburg city centre are easily accessible by car. However, parking can be limited in the city centre, so it's recommended to use public transportation if possible.

By Public Transportation: Gothenburg has an excellent public transportation system. You can use trams and buses to reach Liseberg and other cultural attractions in the city. Visit the Västtrafik website for information on routes, schedules, and tickets.

Availability and Opening Hours: Liseberg's opening hours vary depending on the season. It's best to contact them for the most up-to-date information. Opening hours for other cultural attractions will vary, so it's advisable to contact them

Contact Information: Liseberg can be reached at +46 31 40 01 00.

Address: Liseberg, Örgrytevägen 5, 402 22 Gothenburg.

Unveiling the Natural Wonders of Northern Sweden

Travellers and visitors from all over the globe are drawn to the spectacular natural beauties of northern Sweden. These are some of the natural marvels you may discover in Northern Sweden, which range from enormous wilderness regions to breathtaking vistas and unusual occurrences.

Swedish Lapland:

Swedish Lapland covers a significant portion of northern Sweden and is known for its pristine wilderness. It offers a range of activities and sights such as the mesmerizing Northern Lights (Aurora Borealis) during winter, the Midnight Sun during summer, and the Sami culture. You can also enjoy dog sledging, snowmobiling, ice fishing, and visiting the Icehotel in Jukkasjärvi.

Abisko National Park:

Located in Swedish Lapland, Abisko National Park is famous for its untouched landscapes. The park is home to Mount Njulla, the magnificent Abisko Canyon, and the pristine Lake Torneträsk. It's a popular destination for hiking and skiing, with well-marked trails like the Kungsleden (King's Trail) that stretches for approximately 440 kilometres.

Luleå Archipelago:

Luleå Archipelago is a stunning coastal region dotted with thousands of islands and islets. The archipelago offers opportunities for kayaking, boating, and fishing in the Baltic Sea. In winter, the frozen sea allows for unique experiences like ice skating and snowmobiling.

Jokkmokk Winter Market:

The Jokkmokk Winter Market is a cultural event held annually in Jokkmokk, a small town in Swedish Lapland. It showcases the Sami culture, traditions, and handicrafts. Visitors can experience reindeer sledging, taste Sami cuisine, and purchase traditional Sami crafts.

Kiruna and the Icehotel:

Kiruna and the Icehotel(exterior)

Kiruna and the Icehotel(room)

Kiruna is a town in Swedish Lapland famous for being the gateway to the Arctic and home to the world-renowned Icehotel. This unique hotel is constructed entirely of ice and snow and offers a magical and unforgettable experience for visitors.

Padjelanta National Park:

Padjelanta National Park is one of Sweden's largest national parks and forms part of the UNESCO World Heritage site called Laponia. The park features a vast wilderness, towering mountains, and numerous lakes. Hiking trails lead through the park, offering stunning views of untouched nature.

Stora Sjöfallet National Park:

Located in the province of Norrbotten, Stora Sjöfallet National Park is known for its rugged mountains, roaring waterfalls, and deep valleys. It is a great destination for hiking, camping, and exploring the wild beauty of Northern Sweden.

Sarek National Park:

Sarek National Park is another highlight of Swedish Lapland and is often called "Europe's last wilderness." It is a remote and untouched area, characterized by majestic mountains, glaciers, and winding rivers. Sarek offers challenging hiking routes for experienced adventurers seeking an authentic wilderness experience.

Northern Sweden's natural wonders provide an unparalleled opportunity to connect with nature and experience the unique beauty of this pristine region. Whether you're seeking adventure, relaxation, or cultural immersion, the natural wonders of Northern Sweden will leave you awe-inspired.

Here's a detailed guide on how to reach each natural wonder in Northern Sweden, along with transportation options, availability, opening hours, approximate transportation prices, and contact information:

Swedish Lapland:

To reach Swedish Lapland, you can fly to Kiruna Airport or Luleå Airport, both of which have domestic and international connections.

Availability: Kiruna and Luleå are well-connected by flights and trains from major cities in Sweden.

Opening hours: No specific opening hours.

Transportation price: Flight prices vary based on departure location and season. Train fares depend on the distance travelled.

Contact information: Kiruna Airport - +46 980-190 00, Luleå Airport - +46 920-230 00.

Abisko National Park:

By car: Abisko National Park is located about 95 km west of Kiruna. You can drive from Kiruna along the E10 highway, which takes around 1.5 hours.

By train: The SJ train from Stockholm to Narvik stops at Abisko Turiststation, which is within walking distance of the park entrance.

Availability: Trains operate daily, and road access is available year-round.

Opening hours: The park is accessible 24/7, but visitor centres may have specific opening hours.

Transportation price: Car rental prices vary. Train tickets from Stockholm to Abisko start at around 600 SEK.

Contact information: SJ (train) - +46 771-75 75 75.

Luleå Archipelago:

By car: Luleå is accessible by road via the E4 highway from cities like Stockholm. From Luleå, you can take a boat or ferry to the archipelago islands.

By boat/ferry: Ferries and boat tours are available from Luleå to various islands in the archipelago.

Availability: Boat services operate during the summer season, typically from June to August.

Opening hours: Varies depending on the specific boat or ferry service.

Transportation price: Boat/ferry prices depend on the destination and service provider. Contact them directly for up-to-date pricing.

Contact information: Luleå Tourist Center - +46 920-45 57 00.

Jokkmokk Winter Market:

By car: Jokkmokk is approximately 800 km north of Stockholm, and the journey takes around 10 hours via the E4 and E45 highways.

Availability: Road access is available year-round.

Opening hours: The Jokkmokk Winter Market is an annual event held during the first week of February.

Transportation price: Car rental prices vary. Fuel costs depend on the distance travelled.

Contact information: Jokkmokks Marknad (Jokkmokk Winter Market) - +46 971-222 50.

Kiruna and the Icehotel:

By car: Kiruna is accessible by road via the E10 highway, approximately 1,200 km north of Stockholm. The journey takes around 14 hours.

By train: SJ trains operate from Stockholm to Kiruna regularly.

Availability: Trains and road access are available year-round.

Opening hours: The Icehotel is open year-round, and Kiruna town has various attractions with their operating hours.

Transportation price: Car rental prices vary. Train tickets from Stockholm to Kiruna start at around 700 SEK.

Contact information: Icehotel - +46 980-668 00, Kiruna Tourist Center - +46 980 810 00.

Padjelanta National Park:

By car: Padjelanta National Park is located in the northern part of Swedish Lapland. The park can be reached by car via the E45 highway or the Kungsleden (King's Trail) from Kvikkjokk.

By foot: Hiking is a popular way to access and explore Padjelanta National Park. The Kungsleden trail passes through the park.

Availability: Road access is available year-round, but hiking trails may be more challenging during winter.

Opening hours: The park is accessible 24/7, but visitor centres may have specific opening hours.

Transportation price: Car rental prices vary. Hiking is free, but you may need to pay for camping permits.

Contact information: Swedish Tourist Association (STF) - +46 8-463 22 00.

Stora Sjöfallet National Park:

By car: Stora Sjöfallet National Park is located in the province of Norrbotten. It can be reached by car via the E45 highway or the Kungsleden trail.

By foot: Hiking is the primary mode of exploration within the park.

Availability: Road access is available year-round, but hiking conditions may vary depending on the season.

Opening hours: The park is accessible 24/7, but visitor centres may have specific opening hours.

Transportation price: Car rental prices vary. Hiking is free, but camping permits may be required.

Contact information: Swedish Tourist Association (STF) - +46 8-463 22 00.

Sarek National Park:

By foot: Sarek National Park is a remote wilderness area accessible only by hiking. The main trailhead is at Saltoluokta, which can be reached by boat or helicopter.

Availability: Hiking in Sarek National Park is mainly done during the summer months, from June to September.

Opening hours: The park is accessible 24/7, but visitor centres are not available in the park.

Transportation price: Boat or helicopter prices to reach Saltoluokta vary. Hiking is free, but camping permits may be required.

Contact information: Swedish Tourist Association (STF) - +46 8-463 22 00.

Please note that contact information, availability, and transportation prices are subject to change.

Maps and directions to explore the best of Sweden like a local from your arrival to Sweden to the best accommodation option to the top attraction and hidden gems

---

Exploring Sweden like a local can be an exciting experience!

Here's a detailed guide on how to get to Sweden from various parts of the world, along with directions to the best accommodations and transportation options:

Getting to Sweden:

From Europe: If you're travelling from within Europe, you can easily reach Sweden by air, train, or bus. Major airlines such as SAS, Norwegian, and Ryanair operate flights to Stockholm, Gothenburg, and other cities in Sweden.

From North America: Several airlines offer direct flights from major cities in North America to Stockholm Arlanda Airport, the largest international airport in Sweden. Airlines such as Scandinavian Airlines (SAS), Delta, and United Airlines provide regular services.

From Asia: Airlines like Qatar Airways, Emirates, and Turkish Airlines offer convenient connections from major cities in Asia to Stockholm or Gothenburg. You may have layovers in Doha, Dubai, or Istanbul, depending on the airline and route.

From Australia/New Zealand: Connecting flights from Australia or New Zealand to Stockholm usually have layovers in major Asian hubs like Singapore, Dubai, or Doha. Airlines such as Emirates, Qatar Airways, and Singapore Airlines serve this route.

1. Accommodations in Stockholm:

Stockholm Arlanda Airport

(a) Grand Hotel Stockholm:

This opulent hotel, which dates back to 1874 and is located across the Värtan strait from it, is 2.3 kilometres from the Skansen museum, 1 km from the Moderna Museet, and 6 minutes by foot from Stockholm Palace. There are flat-screen TVs and free Wi-Fi in the cosy, opulent rooms. Suites include living rooms, dining rooms, kitchens, and balconies; some may have access to a private movie theatre or a car service. There is a room service option. There are two elegant restaurants, a cheerful café, an elaborate bar and a classy wine cellar among the amenities. Additionally, there is a spa, an indoor pool, and a fitness centre. Parking, daycare, and meeting space are all chargeable extras.

Grand Hotel Stockholm(exterior)

Grand Hotel Stockholm(room)

Map from
Stockholm Arlanda Airport to Grand Hotel Stockholm
- **Address:** Södra Blasieholmshamnen 8, 103 27 Stockholm, Sweden
- **Transportation:** From Stockholm Arlanda Airport, you can take the Arlanda Express train to Stockholm Central Station. From there, it's a short taxi ride to the Grand Hotel. Alternatively, you can use the

public transportation system, taking the subway to Kungsträdgården station and walking to the hotel.

- **Price:** Prices start at around $300 per night.
- **Contact:** Phone: +46 8 679 35 00
- **Email:** info@grandhotel.se
- **Website:** www.grandhotel.se

(b) Scandic Grand Central:

This upmarket hotel is housed in a stunning structure from the 1880s and is 2.8 kilometres from the Vasa Museum. It is located just across the street from the Oscarsteatern theatre and 6 minutes by foot from Stockholm Central Station. Flat-screen TVs and free WiFi are included in the modest rooms, which have wood flooring and modern bathrooms. Certain have balconies. Upgraded accommodations come with minibars, tea and coffee makers, and classic but elegant décor. Pull-out couches and upscale furniture are added to separate living rooms in suites. There is a breakfast buffet offered. There is an urban-chic bar, an upscale restaurant in a former theatre, and a fashionable café. Additionally, there is a gym and free bike lending.

Scandic Grand Central(Exterior)

Scandic Grand Central(Room)

Map from Stockholm Arlanda Airport to Scandic Grand Central

Address: Kungsgatan 70, 111 20 Stockholm.

Transportation: From Stockholm Arlanda Airport, take the Arlanda Express train to Stockholm Central Station. The Scandic Grand Central is conveniently located next to the station.

Price: Prices start at around $150 per night.

Contact: Phone: +46 8 512 520 00
Email: grandcentral@scandichotels.com
Website: www.scandichotels.com/grandcentral

(c) Nobis Hotel Stockholm:

The Royal Swedish Opera is 9 minutes away by foot, the Royal Palace of Stockholm is 13 minutes away by foot, and the Nordic Museum is 2 km away from this upscale hotel housed in a majestic 19th-century structure. Posh accommodations have flat-screen TVs, minibars, and views of the courtyard, city, or park. Living spaces are added in suites, and some upgraded suites come with Jacuzzi tubs. 24/7 room service is offered. A trendy bar, a spacious lounge, a bistro and an elegant European restaurant are all present. A business centre, a fitness centre, and a sauna are additional features. There is parking and breakfast offered.

Nobis Hotel Stockholm(Exterior)

Nobis Hotel Stockholm(inside)

Nobis Hotel Stockholm(Room)

Map from Stockholm Arlanda Airport to Nobis Hotel Stockholm

Address: Norrmalmstorg 2-4, 111 86 Stockholm.

Transportation: From Stockholm Arlanda Airport, take the Arlanda Express train to Stockholm Central Station. From there, it's a short walk to Nobis Hotel.

Price: Prices start at around $250 per night.

Contact: Phone: +46 8 614 10 00

Email: info@nobishotel.se
Website: https://www.nobishotel.se/
(Note: The prices mentioned are approximate and subject to change. It's advisable to check the respective websites or contact the accommodations for up-to-date rates.)
2. Accommodations in Gothenburg:

Gothenburg
(a) Radisson Blu Riverside Hotel:
The Lindholmspiren ferry pier is 300 metres away from this luxury harborfront hotel, while the Göteborg City Museum is 2 km away. Flat-screen TVs, complimentary Wi-Fi, and tea and coffee makers are included in the stylish rooms. Many have views of the harbour. Nespresso machines and pull-out couches are added to upgraded rooms. Living rooms and balconies are features of suites. 24/7 room service is offered. The boat to Rosenlund runs throughout the workweek. In addition, there are 2 indoor pools, a fitness centre, a business centre, a hip bar and a spa. Parking is available, as well as a rooftop deck.

Radisson Blu Riverside Hotel(outside view)

Radisson Blu Riverside Hotel(Room)

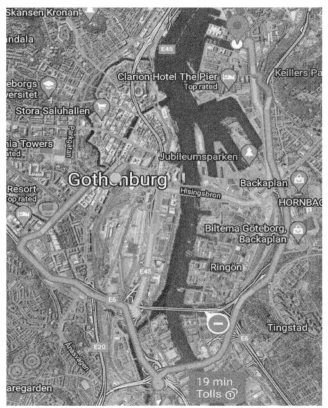

Map from Gothenburg to Radisson Blu Riverside Hotel
Address: Lindholmspiren 4, 417 56 Gothenburg.
Transportation: From Gothenburg Landvetter Airport, you can take the Flygbussarna airport bus directly to the hotel. The bus journey takes approximately 30 minutes.
Price: Prices start at around $150 per night.
Contact: Phone: +46 31 383 40 00
Email: info.riverside.gothenburg@radissonblu.com
Website: www.radissonhotels.com/en-us/hotels/radisson-blu-gothenburg-riverside

(b) Hotel Pigalle:
This upscale hotel, which draws inspiration from Paris in the early 20th century, is a 13-minute walk from the shops and eateries along Kungsportsavenyen's main street.

Additionally, it is a 10-minute walk to the Gothenburg Opera and a kilometre away from the Gothenburg Museum of Art. The opulent rooms include elegant design and furniture, as well as Wi-Fi, flat-screen TVs, and marble bathrooms with elaborate fittings. Room upgrades include sitting spaces. There is a classy restaurant, a chic bar and a seasonally open rooftop patio. Breakfast is offered that is organic.

Hotel Pigalle(exterior)

Hotel Pigalle(Room)

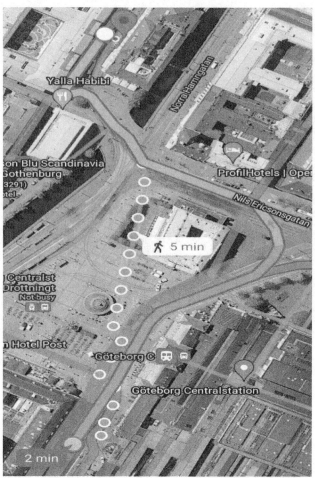

Map from Gothenburg to Hotel Pigalle
Address: Södra Hamngatan 2A, 411 06 Gothenburg.
Transportation: From Gothenburg Landvetter Airport, you can take the Flygbussarna airport bus to Nils Ericson Terminalen. From there, it's a short walk to Hotel Pigalle.
Price: Prices start at around $200 per night.
Contact: Phone: +46 31 80 50 80
Email: info@hotelpigalle.se
Website: www.hotelpigalle.se
(c) Avalon Hotel:

This quirky, stylish hotel is 3 kilometres from Liseberg Amusement Park, 18 minutes on foot from the Gothenburg Museum of Art, and 10 minutes from Gothenburg Central railway station. Free Wi-Fi, flat-screen TVs, minibars, and tea and coffee-making amenities are all provided in modern rooms. Upgraded rooms and suites include living spaces, terraces, or balconies, and some have saunas or exercise facilities. There is a breakfast buffet available. Other features include a chic restaurant/bar with outdoor seating and a rooftop terrace with a glass-bottomed plunge pool.

Avalon Hotel(Exterior)

Avalon Hotel(Room)

Map from Gothenburg to Avalon Hotel
Address: Kungstorget 9, 411 17 Gothenburg.
Transportation: From Gothenburg Landvetter Airport, you can take the Flygbussarna airport bus to Nils Ericson Terminalen. The Avalon Hotel is located within walking distance.
Price: Prices start at around $180 per night.
Contact: Phone: +46 31 751 02 00
Email: info@avalonhotel.se
Website: www.avalonhotel.se

3. Accommodations in Malmö:

Malmö
(a) Story Hotel Studio Malmö:

This chic, modern hotel with views of the resund iminute'stes' walk from Malmö Central Station's trains and 2 km from the Malmö Art Museum. Simple, industrial-chic rooms with complimentary Wi-Fi, smart TVs, minibars, and rainfall showers are available. A sitting area and/or expansive sea views are features of upgraded accommodations. Children under the age of six remain free with an adult. Free breakfast is provided. A rooftop restaurant/bar with views of the city and the strait is among the additional attractions.

Story Hotel Studio Malmö(Exterior)

Story Hotel Studio Malmö(Room)

Map from Malmö central station to Story Hotel Studio Malmö

Address: Tyfongatan 1, 211 19 Malmö, Sweden

Transportation: From Copenhagen Airport (Denmark), you can take the Öresundståg train to Malmö Central Station. The Story Hotel Studio is within walking distance.

Price: Prices start at around $170 per night.

Contact: Phone: +46 40 23 26 00

Email: info@storyhotels.com

Website: www.storyhotels.com/hotels/studio-malmo

(b) Hotel Duxiana Malmö:

This laid-back hotel is conveniently located in the heart of the city, only 4 minutes from Malmö Central Station and 11 minutes from Moderna Museet Malmö. Free Wi-Fi, flat-screen TVs, minifridges, and tea and coffee-making amenities are all included in the comfortable rooms. Suites come with extras like sitting spaces and free-standing bathtubs; some even come with balconies and conference tables. Two conference rooms and a casual restaurant are provided as amenities.

Hotel Duxiana Malmö(Exterior)

Hotel Duxiana Malmö(Premium single room)

Hotel Duxiana Malmö(superior double room)

Map from Malmö to Hotel Duxiana Malmö

Address: Master Johansgatan 1, 211 21 Malmö.

Transportation: From Copenhagen Airport (Denmark), take the Öresundståg train to Malmö Central Station. Hotel Duxiana is located nearby.

Price: Prices start at around $200 per night.

Contact: Phone: +46 40 609 70 00

Email: malmo@duxiana.com

Website: www.duxiana.com/

(c) Clarion Hotel & Congress Malmö Live:

The restaurants on Lilla Torg and Malmö Central Station are both withiminute'sutes walk of this contemporary, high-rise hotel. Malmö Castle may be reached on foot in 11 minutes. Flat-screen TVs and free Wi-Fi are included in the colourful rooms. Some provide city vistas and floor-to-ceiling windows. Sofabeds, sitting spaces, and minifridges are all features in upgraded rooms. Additionally, room service is available round-the-clock. The hotel has a complimentary breakfast buffet. There is a deli, two hip restaurants, one of which serves food with Mexican influences. A bar on the top floor and a gym with a sauna are also there.

Clarion Hotel & Congress Malmö Live(Exterior)

Clarion Hotel & Congress Malmö Live(Room)

Map from Malmö to Clarion Hotel & Congress Malmö Live

Address: Dag Hammarskjölds torg 2, 211 18 Malmö.

Transportation: From Copenhagen Airport (Denmark), take the Öresundståg train to Malmö Central Station. The Clarion Hotel is located adjacent to the station.

Price: Prices start at around $180 per night.

Contact: Phone: +46 40 20 75 00, Email: info@clarionlive.se

Website: https://www.strawberry.se/hotell/sverige/malmo/clarion-hotel-malmo-live/?utm_campaign=gmb-listing&utm_medium=organic&utm_source=google

4. Accommodations in Kiruna:

Kiruna

(a) ICEHOTEL:

This innovative hotel located a mile from both the 18th-century Jukkasjävi Homestead Museum and the Nutti Sámi Siida Cultural and Reindeer Park, is housed in both permanent structures and seasonal ice constructions. Platform beds, heated sleeping bags, and reindeer skins are included in the basic, transient ice cabins; saunas and restrooms are communal. Wi-Fi, flat-screen TVs, and en suite bathrooms are standard in stylish rooms all year round. Cabins come with kitchenettes and living rooms, while permanent ice suites include private saunas. Breakfast is available. A chic restaurant, a cosy lounge and an ice bar are also present. There are also guided tours.

ICEHOTEL(exterior)

ICEHOTEL(Room)

Map from Kiruna to Icehotel
Address: Marknadsvägen 63, 981 91 Jukkasjärvi (Kiruna).
Transportation: From Kiruna Airport, you can take a taxi or arrange a transfer service to ICEHOTEL in Jukkasjärvi, approximately 15 minutes away.
Price: Prices vary depending on the type of accommodation and season. The Ice Rooms start at around $300 per night, while the Art Suites start at around $600 per night.
Contact: Phone: +46 980 66 800
Email: info@icehotel.com

Website: www.icehotel.com

(b) Camp Ripan:

This chic, low-rise hotel is a 14-minute stroll from a bus station, 15 minutes from the Luossavaara ski resort and hiking trail, and 2.3 kilometres from the Luossajärvi lake. The modern cabins, which are scattered across the property and feature modern furniture, include free Wi-Fi, flat-screen TVs, and sitting spaces in addition to minifridges, drying rooms, and ski sheds; some also have fold-away beds and kitchenettes with microwaves. A laid-back restaurant and a stylish spa with an indoor pool, a sauna, and an outdoor hot tub are available as amenities. There are offered activities like reindeer sledging, culinary nights, and tours of the Northern Lights.

Camp Ripan(Exterior)

Camp Ripan(Room)

Map from.Kiruna to Camp Ripan
Address: Campingvägen 5, 981 35 Kiruna.
Transportation: From Kiruna Airport, you can take a taxi or arrange a transfer service to Camp Ripan. The distance is approximately 10 minutes by car.
Price: Prices start at around $150 per night for a standard cabin.
Contact: Phone: +46 980 630 00
Email: info@ripan.se
Website: www.ripan.se
(Note: It's recommended to check the respective accommodation websites or contact them directly for up-to-date prices and availability.)
Transportation prices within Sweden may vary depending on the mode of transportation and distance. As an estimate, here are some common transportation costs:

- **Arlanda Express train from Stockholm Arlanda Airport to Stockholm Central Station:** Approximately $30-$40 per person.
- **Flygbussarna airport bus from Gothenburg Landvetter Airport to Gothenburg city centre:** Approximately $15-$20 per person.
- **Öresundståg train from Copenhagen Airport to Malmö Central Station:** Approximately $15-$25 per person.
- **Taxi from Kiruna Airport to accommodations in Kiruna:** Approximately $20-$30.

Please note that the prices mentioned are approximate and subject to change.
A detailed description of each attraction and hidden gem in Sweden, including what visitors can see, experience, and other important information:

Stockholm:
(a) Royal Palace (Kungliga Slottet):

The Royal Palace is a magnificent landmark in Stockholm and the official residence of the Swedish royal family. Visitors can explore the stunning Royal Apartments, the Royal Chapel, and the Treasury. The Changing of the Guard ceremony is also a popular attraction. The palace offers a glimpse into Swedish history and regal splendour.
(b) Vasa Museum:

The Vasa Museum is home to the Vasa warship, which
sank on its maiden voyage in 1628 and was salvaged
centuries later. The museum showcases the incredibly

preserved ship, along with exhibitions and displays that provide insight into life during the 17th century. It's a unique and fascinating experience for history and maritime enthusiasts.

(c) Gamla Stan (Old Town):

Gamla Stan is Stockholm's historic old town, characterized by narrow cobblestone streets, colourful buildings, and medieval architecture. Visitors can wander through the charming alleys, explore the Royal Palace, visit the Stockholm Cathedral, and browse shops selling traditional Swedish handicrafts. The area also offers a range of cosy cafes and restaurants to enjoy local cuisine.

(d) Drottningholm Palace:

Drottningholm Palace is a UNESCO World Heritage site and the private residence of the Swedish royal family. The palace features beautiful gardens, the Chinese Pavilion, and the Drottningholm Palace Theatre, which hosts opera and theatre performances. Visitors can take guided tours of the palace, stroll through the formal gardens, and enjoy the tranquil surroundings.

Gothenburg:

(a) Liseberg Amusement Park:

Liseberg is a popular amusement park offering thrilling rides, entertainment, and attractions for all ages. From roller coasters to carousels, the park has a wide range of attractions. Liseberg also hosts concerts, shows, and cultural events throughout the year, making it a lively and exciting destination for families and thrill-seekers.

(b) Universeum:

Universeum is a science centre and museum where visitors can explore the wonders of the natural world. The exhibits include a rainforest, a coral reef, a space exhibition, and an aquarium. Some interactive displays and activities educate and engage visitors of all ages, making it a perfect destination for science enthusiasts and curious minds.

(c) Haga District:

Haga is a charming district known for its 19th-century wooden houses, picturesque streets, and cosy cafes. It's an ideal place to wander and soak in the laid-back atmosphere. Visitors can explore unique shops selling antiques, vintage items, and local handicrafts. Don't miss the chance to try a traditional Swedish "fika" (coffee break) with delicious pastries at one of the quaint cafes.

(d) Gothenburg Archipelago (Southern Islands):

The Gothenburg Archipelago is a hidden gem of picturesque islands and stunning natural beauty. Visitors can take a ferry to explore the islands, which offer opportunities for swimming, hiking, and enjoying the serene coastal landscapes. Some islands have charming fishing villages and excellent seafood restaurants, allowing visitors to experience the traditional coastal culture of Sweden.

Malmö:
(a) Turning Torso:

Turning Torso is an iconic skyscraper and architectural marvel that dominates the skyline of Malmö. Designed by Santiago Calatrava, it is the tallest building in Scandinavia. While not open to the public, its twisting form and unique design make it a must-see sight. Visitors can marvel at the impressive structure from the outside and capture stunning photos of this modern landmark.

(b) Malmö Castle (Malmöhus Castle):

Malmö Castle, also known as Malmöhus Castle, is a well-preserved fortress from the 16th century. It houses several museums, including the Malmö Art Museum and the Natural History Museum. Visitors can explore the castle's history, stroll through the beautiful gardens, and admire the exhibitions. The castle also hosts cultural events and temporary exhibitions, offering a diverse range of experiences.

(c) Ribersborg Beach (Ribersborgsstranden):

Ribersborg Beach is a popular sandy beach located near the city centre of Malmö. It offers a relaxing atmosphere and panoramic views of the Öresund Bridge. Visitors can enjoy sunbathing, swimming in the Baltic Sea, and taking leisurely walks along the waterfront promenade. There are also facilities such as restaurants and cafes nearby, making it a great spot to unwind and enjoy the coastal scenery.

(d) Malmö Saluhall:

Malmö Saluhall is a vibrant food market that showcases the rich culinary traditions of Sweden. Visitors can explore a variety of stalls offering fresh produce, local delicacies, gourmet products, and international flavours. It's a great place to sample Swedish dishes, buy high-quality ingredients, or simply soak in the bustling atmosphere of the market. The hall also hosts occasional food events and tastings, adding to the culinary experience.

Kiruna:

(a) Icehotel:

The Icehotel in Jukkasjärvi is a unique accommodation made entirely of ice and snow. Visitors can experience the stunning ice sculptures, stay in ice rooms, and even witness the creation of the hotel each year. The Icehotel also offers activities such as ice sculpting, snowmobiling, and dog sledging, allowing visitors to immerse themselves in the winter wonderland of Swedish Lapland.

(b) Abisko National Park:

Abisko National Park is a pristine wilderness with breathtaking landscapes. Visitors can hike along well-marked trails, explore the stunning Torneträsk Lake, and marvel at the Northern Lights during the winter months. The park is known for its diverse flora and fauna, making it a haven for nature lovers, photographers, and outdoor enthusiasts.

(c) Kiruna Church:

Kiruna Church is an architectural masterpiece and a symbol of the town's history. The wooden church, known for its unique design and intricate details, offers a serene atmosphere for visitors to admire its beauty and experience a moment of tranquillity. The church also hosts regular services and occasional concerts, providing a glimpse into the local community and culture.

(d) Kiruna Mine (LKAB Visitor Center):

The Kiruna Mine, operated by LKAB, is one of the world's largest underground iron ore mines. The visitor centre provides insights into the mining industry and its significance for the region. Visitors can learn about the mining process, explore interactive exhibitions, and even take a guided tour to witness the impressive scale of the operations. It offers a fascinating glimpse into the industrial heritage of Kiruna.

Each attraction and hidden gem in Sweden offers a unique experience, whether it's delving into history and culture, indulging in thrilling activities, or immersing oneself in the natural beauty of the country. Visitors can choose their preferred destinations based on their interests and create unforgettable memories during their exploration of Sweden.

The top attractions and hidden gems provided in Sweden, along with transportation options directions prices and contact information:

Stockholm:

(a) Royal Palace (Kungliga Slottet):

Address: Kungliga slottet, 107 70 Stockholm, Sweden.

Transportation: Located in the heart of Stockholm, the Royal Palace is easily accessible on foot from most city centre locations.

Price: The entrance fee for adults is approximately $15.

Contact: Phone: +46 8 402 61 00

Website: www.kungligaslotten.se

(b) Vasa Museum:

Address: Galärvarvsvägen 14, 115 21 Stockholm, Sweden.

Transportation: Take the ferry or bus to Djurgården from the city centre. The Vasa Museum is a short walk from the ferry/bus stop.

Price: The entrance fee for adults is approximately $20.

Contact: Phone: +46 8 519 548 80

Email: vasamuseet@maritima.se

Website: www.vasamuseet.se

(c) Gamla Stan (Old Town):

Address: Stadsholmen, 111 29 Stockholm, Sweden.

Transportation: Gamla Stan is within walking distance from the city centre. You can also take the subway to Gamla Stan station.

Price: Free to explore, but costs may apply for specific attractions or dining.

Contact: +46 8 508 285 08

Website: https://www.visitstockholm.com/o/gamla-stan/

(d) Drottningholm Palace:

Address: Drottningholms Slott Slottsstallet 11, 178 93 Drottningholm, Sweden
Transportation: Take a ferry from Stockholm City Hall (Strömkajen) to Drottningholm Palace. The ferry ride takes approximately 50 minutes.
Price: The entrance fee for adults is approximately $15.
Contact: Phone: +46 8 402 61 00
Email: info@royalcourt.se
Website: https://www.kungligaslotten.se/vara-besoksmal/drottningholms-slott.html
Gothenburg:
(a) Liseberg Amusement Park:
Address: Örgrytevägen 5, 402 22 Gothenburg.
Transportation: Take tram line 5 or bus 55 to Liseberg station.
Price: The entrance fee varies depending on the season and attractions chosen. Prices start at approximately $40.
Contact: Phone: +46 31 400 100
Email: info@liseberg.se
Website: www.liseberg. se
(b) Universeum:
Address: Södra Vägen 50, 412 54 Göteborg, Sweden
Transportation: Universeum is located near Korsvägen. Take tram lines 2, 4, 5, 6, 7, 8, or 13 to Korsvägen.
Price: The entrance fee for adults is approximately $30.
Contact: Phone: +46 31 335 64 00
Email: info@universeum.se
Website: www.universeum.se
(c) Haga District:
Address: Haga Nygata, 413 01 Gothenburg.
Transportation: Haga is within walking distance from the city centre of Gothenburg. You can also take tram lines 3, 9, or 11 to Järntorget and walk to Haga.

Price: Free to explore, but costs may apply for shopping or dining.

Contact: No specific contact information.

(d) Gothenburg Archipelago (Southern Islands):

Address: The southern archipelago of Gothenburg.

Transportation: Take a ferry from Saltholmen terminal, which is accessible by tram lines 9 and 11. Ferries connect to various islands in the archipelago.

Price: Ferry tickets vary depending on the destination. Prices start at approximately $10.

Contact: Phone: +46 31 350 01 01

Website:
https://www.gothenburgtours.se/?gclid=Cj0KCAjwhJukBh
BPEi0AniIcNb7S19M699zPLTJHWUkuvRpm79ZcXAE
YLaipovInCrArY7CWZpc4xWIaAoCVEALw_wcB

Malmö:

(a) Turning Torso:

Address: Lilla Varvsgatan 14, 211 15 Malmö.

Transportation: Turning Torso is located in the Västra Hamnen area. It is easily accessible by bus or train from the city centre.

Price: It's not open to the public, but you can admire it from the outside for free.

Contact: Phone: +46 40 17 45 00

Website: https://www.hsb.se/malmo/om-
boende/hyreslagenhet/turning-torso--malmos-
landmarke/

(b) Malmö Castle (Malmöhus Castle):

Address: Malmöhusvägen 6, 211 18 Malmö.

Transportation: Malmö Castle is located near Malmö Central Station, within walking distance from the city centre.

Price: The entrance fee for adults is approximately $10.

Contact: Phone: +46 40 34 10 00
Email: malmo.museum@malmo.se
Website: www.malmomuseer.se

(c) Ribersborg Beach (Ribersborgsstranden):
Address: Limhamnsvägen 35, 217 59 Malmö.
Transportation: Take bus number 2 from the city centre to the Ribersborg stop. It's a short walk from there to the beach.
Price: Free to visit and enjoy the beach.
Contact: No specific contact information.

(d) Malmö Saluhall:
Address: Gibraltargatan 6, 211 18 Malmö.
Transportation: Malmö Saluhall is located near Malmö Central Station, within walking distance from the city centre.
Price: Free to enter, but costs may apply for purchases.
Contact: Phone: +46 40 12 49 00
Email: info@malmostad.se
Website: www.malmosaluhall.se

Kiruna:
(a) Icehotel:
Address: Marknadsvägen 63, 981 91 Jukkasjärvi.
Transportation: From Kiruna, you can take a taxi or arrange a transfer service to Icehotel in Jukkasjärvi, approximately 20 minutes away.
Price: Prices vary depending on the experience or activity. Guided tours start at approximately $30.
Contact: Phone: +46 980 668 00
Email: info@icehotel.com
Website: www.icehotel.com

(b) Abisko National Park:
Address: Abisko National Park, 981 07 Abisko.

Transportation: Take a train from Kiruna to Abisko Turiststation. The journey takes approximately 1 hour.
Price: The entrance to the national park is free, but costs may apply for activities or guided tours.
Contact: Phone: +46 920 960 00
Email: info@abiskonaturum.se
Website: www.abisko.nu
(c) Kiruna Church:
Address: Föreningsgatan 8, 981 34 Kiruna.
Transportation: Kiruna Church is located in the city centre and is easily accessible on foot from most accommodations in Kiruna.
Price: Free to visit.
Contact: Phone: +46 980 678 00
Email: kiruna.forsamling@svenskakyrkan.se
Website: www.svenskakyrkan.se/kiruna
(d) Kiruna Mine (LKAB Visitor Center):
Address: 17, Lars Janssonsgatan, 981 31 Kiruna, Sweden.
Transportation: Kiruna Mine is located in the city centre and is easily accessible on foot from most accommodations in Kiruna.
Price: The entrance fee for adults is approximately $15.
Contact: Phone: +46 980 825 80
Email: besok@lkab.com
Website: https://kirunalapland.se/aktiviteter/lkabs-visitor-centre/
Please note that transportation prices may vary depending on the mode of transportation and distance.
As an estimate, here are some common transportation costs within Sweden:
- **Public transportation within cities (bus, tram, or metro):** Approximately $2-$4 per trip.

- **Train tickets between cities (e.g., Stockholm to Gothenburg):** Prices vary based on distance and time of booking. Approximately $50-$100 per person.

It's recommended to check with the respective attractions or transportation providers for the most accurate and up-to-date information regarding prices, schedules, and availability.

Enjoy exploring the top attractions and hidden gems in Sweden!

Perfect itinerary options to explore Sweden like a local

Exploring Sweden like a local can be a wonderful experience.

Here are 3 days to 1-month itinerary options to help you discover the best of Sweden and immerse yourself in its culture and natural beauty:

3 Days Itinerary:

Day 1:

- Start your journey in Stockholm. From Stockholm Central Station, head south on Vasagatan and continue onto Kungsgatan to reach Gamla Stan (Old Town).
- The Royal Palace (Kungliga Slottet) is located at Slottsbacken 1, 111 30 Stockholm. It is open daily from 10:00 AM to 5:00 PM. The admission fee is

approximately 160 SEK ($18.70 USD) for adults and 80 SEK ($9.35 USD) for children.

- **Contact information: Phone:** +46 8 402 61 00.

Day 2:

- Take a day trip to Uppsala by train from Stockholm Central Station. Trains depart frequently, and the journey takes approximately 40 minutes. The one-way ticket price is around 80 SEK ($9.35 USD).

Uppsala

Uppsala Cathedral (Domkyrkan)

- Uppsala Cathedral (Domkyrkan) is located at Domkyrkoplan, 753 10 Uppsala. It is open for visitors from 9:00 AM to 5:00 PM. There is no entrance fee, but a donation is appreciated.
- **Contact information: Phone:** +46 18 430 35 00.
- **Website:** https://www.svenskakyrkan.se/uppsaladomkyrka

Day 3:

- Head to Gothenburg by train from Stockholm Central Station. The journey takes around 3 hours. The one-way ticket price varies depending on the class and booking time, starting from approximately 500 SEK ($58.40 USD).

Liseberg amusement park

- Visit Liseberg amusement park, located at Örgrytevägen 5, 402 22 Gothenburg. The park's opening hours and availability may vary, so it's advisable to check their website for the latest information. Ticket prices range from 110 SEK ($12.88 USD) to 495 SEK ($57.88 USD), depending on age and the type of pass you choose.
- **Contact information: Phone:** +46 31 40 01 00
- Website: https://www.liseberg.se/

5 Days Itinerary:

Days 1-3: Follow the 3-day itinerary mentioned above for Stockholm, Uppsala, and Gothenburg.

Day 4:

Öckerö

- Take a ferry from Gothenburg to Öckerö. The ferry departs from Lilla Varholmen, which is approximately a 20-minute drive from central Gothenburg. The ferry ticket price is around 50 SEK ($5.85 USD) for a one-way trip.

Day 5:

- Return to Gothenburg by ferry from Öckerö. From Gothenburg Central Station, take a train to Malmö Central Station. The journey takes around 3 hours. The one-way ticket price starts from approximately 350 SEK ($40.95 USD).

7 Days Itinerary:

Days 1-3: Follow the 3-day itinerary mentioned above for Stockholm, Uppsala, and Gothenburg.

Day 4:

- Take a ferry from Gothenburg to Öckerö. The ferry departs from Lilla Varholmen, which is approximately a 20-minute drive from central

Gothenburg. The ferry ticket price is around 50 SEK ($5.85 USD) for a one-way trip.

Day 5:

- Return to Gothenburg by ferry from Öckerö.

Gothenburg Central Station

Gothenburg Central Station

Malmö Central Station

Malmö Central Station

Malmö Central Station
- Take a train from Gothenburg Central Station to Malmö Central Station. The journey takes around 3 hours. The one-way ticket price starts from approximately 350 SEK ($40.95 USD).
- **Website:** https://www.jernhusen.se/hitta-din-station/goteborg-centralstation/

Day 6:

Turning Torso
- Explore Malmö, including attractions like the Turning Torso and the Old Town.
- Contact: Phone: +46 40 17 45 00
- Website: https://www.hsb.se/malmo/om-boende/hyreslagenhet/turning-torso--malmos-landmarke/

Moderna Museet Malmö

- Consider visiting the Moderna Museet Malmö or the Malmö Castle (Malmöhus Castle), depending on your interests. Check their websites for opening hours, admission fees, and availability.
- **Contact: Phone:** +46 40 685 79 37

- **Website:**
  https://www.modernamuseet.se/malmo/sv/

Day 7:

- Take a train from Malmö Central Station to Copenhagen, Denmark. The journey takes around 30 minutes. The one-way ticket price starts from approximately 120 SEK ($14.03 USD).

Nyhavn

Little Mermaid statue

Tivoli Gardens

- Spend the day exploring Copenhagen's highlights, such as Nyhavn(it is a cool place with a lot of colourful buildings), the Little Mermaid statue, and Tivoli Gardens.

2 Weeks Itinerary:

Days 1-7: Follow the 7-day itinerary mentioned above for Stockholm, Uppsala, Gothenburg, Öckerö, Malmö, Visby, and Copenhagen.

Day 8-14:

- Take a flight from Copenhagen to Kiruna. Flight prices and availability may vary, so it's recommended to check with airlines like SAS or Norwegian for the most up-to-date information.
- Explore Kiruna and Swedish Lapland, including attractions like Abisko National Park and the Icehotel in Jukkasjärvi. Check the top attractions and hidden gems chapter for websites, opening hours, availability, and pricing.

1 Month Itinerary:

Days 1-14: Follow the 2-week itinerary mentioned above for Stockholm, Uppsala, Gothenburg, Öckerö, Malmö, Visby, Copenhagen, Kiruna, Abisko National Park, and the Icehotel.

Days 15-21:

Höga Kusten Tourism AB
Contact: Phone: +46 77 126 50 00
Website: https://www.hogakusten.com/sv

- From Kiruna, travel to the High Coast (Höga Kusten) area. Take a train from Kiruna Station to Örnsköldsvik Station. The journey takes approximately 9 hours, with a transistor in Umeå. The one-way ticket price starts from around 600 SEK ($70.20 USD).

Skuleskogen National Park

Skuleskogen National Park

Skuleskogen National Park

- Explore the stunning coastal landscapes and nature reserves of the High Coast, including Skuleskogen National Park and the Höga Kusten Bridge.

Ulvön

Trysunda

- Consider taking a boat tour to explore the archipelago and visit islands like Ulvön or Trysunda.

Days 22-28:

Mariefred

- From the High Coast, travel to Mariefred. Take a train from Örnsköldsvik Station to Mariefred Station. The journey takes approximately 8 hours, with transfers in Umeå and Stockholm. The one-way ticket price starts from around 500 SEK ($58.40 USD).

Gripsholm Castle
Contact: Phone: +46 159 101 94
Website: https://www.kungligaslotten.se/vara-besoksmal/gripsholms-slott.html

- Explore Mariefred, a picturesque town known for Gripsholm Castle. Visit the castle and take a stroll along the charming streets.

Days 29-30:

- Return to Stockholm from Mariefred. Take a train from Mariefred Station to Stockholm Central Station. The journey takes approximately 1 hour and 30 minutes. The one-way ticket price starts from around 100 SEK ($11.68 USD).
- Spend your last days in Stockholm revisiting your favorite spots or exploring new areas of the city.

Please note that transportation prices, availability, and fees may vary and are subject to change. It's advisable to check the respective websites or contact the transportation providers for the most up-to-date information. Additionally, for accommodations, it's recommended to book in advance and check availability based on your preferred travel dates.

Museums and Galleries to Visit in Sweden

Here's an overview of each museum and gallery, including what they are about and what visitors can expect to enjoy:

Vasa Museum (Stockholm):

The Vasa Museum is dedicated to the Vasa ship, a 17th-century warship that sank on its maiden voyage and was salvaged centuries later. The museum showcases the

remarkably well-preserved ship and provides insights into maritime history. Visitors can explore the ship's exhibits, watch a film about its history, and learn about life at sea during the period.
Contact: Phone: +46 8 519 548 80
Address: Galärvarvsvägen 14, 115 21 Stockholm, Sweden
Website: https://www.vasamuseet.se/
Availability: Tuesday 10 am to 5 pm, Wednesday 10 am to 8 pm and Thursday through Monday 8:30 am to 6 pm
Skansen Open-Air Museum (Stockholm):

Skansen is the world's first open-air museum and features traditional Swedish architecture, historic buildings, and a zoo. Visitors can stroll through the beautifully preserved structures, participate in traditional crafts and activities, and interact with animals native to Scandinavia. Skansen offers a glimpse into Swedish culture, history, and wildlife.
Contact: Phone: +46 8 442 80 00
Address: Djurgårdsslätten 49-51, 115 21 Stockholm, Sweden

Website: https://skansen.se/en/
Availability: Monday through Sunday 10 am to 6 pm
ABBA: The Museum (Stockholm, Gothenburg, Umeå):

ABBA: The Museum celebrates the iconic Swedish pop group ABBA. Visitors can explore interactive exhibits, listen to their music, see their costumes, and even step on stage with a hologram of the band. The museum offers a fun and nostalgic experience for fans of ABBA and music lovers in general.

Contact: Address: Djurgårdsvägen 68, 115 21 Stockholm, Sweden

Website: https://abbathemuseum.com/en/

Availability: Monday through Sunday 10 am to 6 pm

Museum of Modern Art (Stockholm):

The Museum of Modern Art in Stockholm showcases contemporary art from both Swedish and international artists. Visitors can admire a diverse range of art forms, including paintings, sculptures, photography, and installations. The museum often hosts temporary exhibitions, providing a dynamic and ever-changing art experience.

Contact: Phone: +46 8 520 235 00
Address: Exercisplan 4, 111 49 Stockholm, Sweden
Website: https://www.modernamuseet.se/stockholm/sv/
Availability: Friday and Tuesday 10 am to 8 pm, Saturday and Sunday 10 am to 6 pm, Wednesday and Thursday 10 am to 6 pm and closed on Monday
National Museum (Stockholm):

The National Museum is the largest art museum in Sweden, housing a vast collection of artworks spanning centuries. Visitors can explore Swedish and European art, including paintings, sculptures, and decorative art. The museum offers a comprehensive overview of art history, from the Middle Ages to contemporary works.

Contact: Phone: +46 8 519 543 00

Address: Södra Blasieholmshamnen 2, 111 48 Stockholm, Sweden

Website: https://www.nationalmuseum.se/

Availability: Closed on Monday and Tuesday, Wednesday to Friday 11 am to 5 pm, Saturday and Sunday 10 am to 5 pm

Gothenburg Museum of Art (Gothenburg):

The Gothenburg Museum of Art features an extensive collection of Nordic and European art from the 15th century onwards. Visitors can appreciate works by renowned artists such as Rembrandt, Monet, and Picasso. The museum also showcases contemporary art and hosts temporary exhibitions.

Contact: Phone: +46 31 368 35 00
Address: Götaplatsen 6, 412 56 Göteborg, Sweden
Website: https://goteborgskonstmuseum.se/
Availability: Tuesday to Sunday 11 am to 5 pm
Uppsala Cathedral Treasury (Uppsala):

The Uppsala Cathedral Treasury is located within Uppsala Cathedral and houses a collection of ecclesiastical treasures. Visitors can view exquisite religious artefacts, including gold and silver objects, textiles, and manuscripts. The treasury provides insights into the history and religious heritage of Uppsala.

Contact: Phone: +46 18 430 35 00

Address: Domkyrkoplan, 753 10 Uppsala, Sweden

Website:

https://www.svenskakyrkan.se/uppsaladomkyrka

Availability: Monday to Sunday 8 am to 6 pm

Gotland Museum (Visby):

The Gotland Museum focuses on the cultural and natural history of the island of Gotland. Visitors can explore archaeological finds, historical artefacts, and exhibits on local folklore. The museum provides a comprehensive understanding of the island's rich heritage and its significance in Swedish history.

Contact: Phone: +46 498 29 27 00
Address: Strandgatan 14, 621 56 Visby, Sweden
Website: https://www.gotlandsmuseum.se/
Availability: Monday 10 am to 6 pm
Museum of World Culture (Gothenburg):

The Museum of World Culture offers thought-provoking exhibitions that explore themes of global culture, diversity, and social issues. Visitors can engage with interactive displays, multimedia installations, and contemporary art.

The museum encourages reflection and dialogue on topics of global significance.
Contact: Phone: +46 10 456 12 00
Address: Södra Vägen 54, 412 54 Göteborg, Sweden
Website: https://www.varldskulturmuseet.se/
Availability: Tuesday to Sunday 11 am to 5 pm
Museum of Mediterranean and Near Eastern Antiquities (Stockholm):

The Museum of Mediterranean and Near Eastern Antiquities showcases artefacts from ancient civilizations in the Mediterranean and Near East. Visitors can admire Egyptian mummies, Greek and Roman sculptures, and intricate ancient jewellery. The museum offers a fascinating journey through ancient history and cultures.
Contact: Phone: +46 10 456 12 98
Address: Fredsgatan 2, 111 52 Stockholm, Sweden
Website: https://www.medelhavsmuseet.se/
Availability: 11 am to 8 pm

Swedish History Museum (Stockholm):

The Swedish History Museum provides an in-depth look into Sweden's history, from prehistoric times to the present day. Visitors can explore exhibitions featuring Viking artefacts, medieval treasures, and interactive displays that bring Sweden's past to life.

Contact: Phone: +46 8 519 556 00
Address: Narvavägen 13-17, 114 84 Stockholm, Sweden
Website: https://historiska.se/
Availability: Tuesday to Sunday 10 am to 5 pm
Malmö Konsthall (Malmö):

Malmö Konsthall is a contemporary art gallery that hosts exhibitions by Swedish and international artists. The gallery showcases a variety of artistic mediums, including painting, sculpture, video art, and installations. It's a vibrant space that encourages dialogue and engagement with contemporary art.

Contact: Phone: +46 40 34 60 00

Address: S:t Johannesgatan 7, 205 80 Malmö, Sweden

Website: https://malmokonsthall.se/

Availability: Tuesday to Sunday 11 am to 5 pm

Museum of Ethnography (Stockholm):

The Museum of Ethnography focuses on the cultural diversity and traditions of different peoples around the world. It houses collections of objects, photographs, and multimedia presentations that explore various cultural practices, rituals, and artefacts.

Contact: Phone: +46 10 456 12 99

Address: Djurgårdsbrunnsvägen 34, 115 27 Stockholm, Sweden

Website: https://www.etnografiskamuseet.se/

Availability: Tuesday to Sunday 11 am to 5 pm

Each of these museums and galleries offers a unique experience, providing insights into different aspects of art, history, culture, and contemporary issues. Make sure to check their websites for specific exhibitions, events, and additional information that may enhance your visit. Enjoy your exploration of these wonderful cultural institutions in Sweden!

Enjoying Sports and Outdoor Activities in Sweden

Sweden offers a plethora of sports and outdoor activities that travellers and tourists can enjoy.

Here are some popular activities, along with their locations, directions, fees (if applicable), and other essential information:

Skiing and Snowboarding in Åre:

Location: Åre is a popular ski resort town located in central Sweden.

Directions: From Stockholm, you can take a flight to Åre Östersund Airport or a train to Åre Train Station.

Fees: Lift pass fees vary depending on the duration and time of year. It is best to check the Åre ski resort website for up-to-date pricing information.

Other important information: Equipment rental is available in Åre, and there are numerous accommodations, restaurants, and après-ski options in the area.

Contact: Phone: +46 77 184 00 00

Address: Trondheimsleden 52, 837 52 Åre, Sweden

Website: https://www.skistar.com/sv/vara-skidorter/are/vinter-i-are/

Hiking in Abisko National Park:

Location: Abisko National Park is situated in northern Sweden, near the town of Kiruna.

Directions: From Kiruna, you can take a bus or drive to Abisko National Park. There are also train connections available from Stockholm to Abisko Turiststation.

Fees: There is no entrance fee to enter Abisko National Park.

Other important information: Abisko is renowned for its stunning landscapes, including the famous Lapporten mountain formation and the Northern Lights during winter. It's advisable to bring appropriate hiking gear, including sturdy shoes and warm clothing.

Contact: Phone: +46 920 960 00

Address: Kiruna, Sweden

Website:
https://www.lansstyrelsen.se/norrbotten/besoksmal/nationalparker/abisko.html?sv.target=12.382c024b1800285d5863a897&sv.12.382c024b1800285d5863a897.route=/&searchString=&counties=&municipalities=&reserveTypes=&natureTypes=&accessibility=&facilities=&sort=none

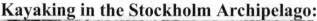

Kayaking in the Stockholm Archipelago:

Location: The Stockholm Archipelago consists of thousands of islands stretching east of Stockholm, the capital city of Sweden.

Directions: From Stockholm, you can take a public ferry or rent a kayak from various locations in the city to explore the archipelago.

Fees: Rental fees for kayaks vary depending on the provider and duration. Public ferry fees can be found on the Waxholmsbolaget website.

Other important information: It's recommended to have some kayaking experience before venturing into the archipelago. Check the weather forecast and sea conditions before setting out, and be aware of any restricted areas or wildlife sanctuaries.

Address: Strömparterren 1, 111 30 Stockholm, Sweden

Website: http://www.paddlingstockholm.se/

Cycling in Gotland:

Location: Gotland is a large Swedish island located in the Baltic Sea.

Directions: You can reach Gotland by taking a ferry from Nynäshamn or Oskarshamn on the Swedish mainland.

Fees: Ferry fees for passengers and bicycles can be found on the ferry company's website.

Other important information: Gotland offers beautiful cycling routes with varying terrain and scenic coastal landscapes. There are bike rental options available on the island, and it's advisable to bring a map or use a GPS navigation device to explore the different cycling trails.

Contact: Phone: +46 498 21 41 33

Address: Skeppsbron 2, 621 57 Visby, Sweden

Website: https://gotlandscykeluthyrning.com/

Fishing in the Mörrum River:

Location: The Mörrum River is situated in southern Sweden, near the town of Karlshamn.

Directions: You can reach the Mörrum River by taking a train to Mörrum Station or driving to the nearby area.

Fees: Fishing permits are required and can be purchased online or at designated outlets. Prices vary depending on the duration and type of fishing.

Other important information: The Mörrum River is famous for its salmon fishing, attracting anglers from around the world. Make sure to familiarize yourself with the local fishing regulations, catch-and-release policies, and any specific fishing seasons.

Contact: Phone: +46 70 671 22 86

Address: Laxens Hus, 375 21 Mörrum, Sweden

Rock Climbing in Kullaberg Nature Reserve:

Location: Kullaberg Nature Reserve is situated on the west coast of Sweden, near the town of Mölle.

Directions: From Helsingborg, you can drive or take a bus to Kullaberg Nature Reserve.

Fees: There is no entrance fee to access the nature reserve. However, some climbing areas may require a permit, which can be obtained from the Kullaberg Nature Reserve Visitor Center for a small fee.

Other important information: Kullaberg offers a variety of rock climbing routes for both beginners and experienced climbers. It's recommended to bring your climbing gear, including ropes, harnesses, and helmets.

Contact: Phone: +46 70 716 25 50

Address: Fjällbackagatan 3, 263 58 Höganäs, Sweden

Website: https://www.klattringpakullaberg.se/

Wildlife Safari in the Swedish Lapland:

Location: The Swedish Lapland covers the northern part of Sweden, including towns like Kiruna and Jokkmokk.

Directions: You can reach the Swedish Lapland by flying to Kiruna Airport or taking a train to Kiruna or Jokkmokk.

Fees: The fees for wildlife safaris may vary depending on the operator and the duration of the tour. It's best to check with local tour companies for pricing information.

Other important information: The Swedish Lapland is home to a diverse range of wildlife, including reindeer, moose, arctic foxes, and even the elusive wolverines. Joining a guided wildlife safari allows you to explore the region's natural beauty while learning about the local fauna.

Contact: Phone: +46 73 914 04 72

Address: Carlsberg 1, 921 97 Lycksele, Sweden
Website: https://www.wildlapland.se/
Sailing in the Göta Canal:

Location: The Göta Canal stretches across Sweden, connecting Stockholm on the east coast to Gothenburg on the west coast.

Directions: You can reach different sections of the Göta Canal by train, bus, or car, depending on the starting point and desired destination.

Fees: The fees for sailing or cruising the Göta Canal depend on the type of vessel, duration, and services included. It's advisable to contact canal cruise operators or boat rental companies for specific pricing details.

Other important information: The Göta Canal offers a unique opportunity to explore Sweden's scenic landscapes and historic waterways. Whether you choose to rent a sailboat or join a guided canal cruise, you'll be able to enjoy picturesque views, charming locks, and historic sites along the canal.

Contact: Phone: +46 70 546 91 69

Address: Svarta gatan 1, 591 46 Motala, Sweden

Website: https://gotakanalcharter.se/

Golfing in Barsebäck Golf & Country Club:

Location: Barsebäck Golf & Country Club is located near the town of Löddeköpinge in southern Sweden.

Directions: From Malmö, you can drive or take a train to reach Barsebäck Golf & Country Club.

Fees: The green fees at Barsebäck Golf & Country Club vary depending on the season, time of day, and whether you're a member or visitor. It's recommended to check their website for up-to-date pricing information.

Other important information: Barsebäck Golf & Country Club offers two 18-hole championship golf courses and is renowned for hosting international golf tournaments. The club also provides facilities such as a driving range, a golf shop, and dining options.

Contact: Phone: +46 46 77 70 60

Address: Klubbhusvägen 5, 246 55 Löddeköpinge, Sweden
Website: https://barseback.com/
Horseback Riding in Dalarna:

Location: Dalarna is a region located in central Sweden, known for its picturesque landscapes and traditional Swedish culture.

Directions: From Stockholm, you can reach Dalarna by train or car. The region has several towns and villages where horseback riding is offered, such as Mora, Rättvik, and Leksand.

Fees: The fees for horseback riding in Dalarna vary depending on the duration and type of ride, as well as the specific stable or equestrian centre. It's best to contact local riding schools or tour operators for pricing details.

Other important information: Horseback riding in Dalarna allows you to explore the region's forests, lakes, and charming countryside. Some riding centres offer guided tours suitable for riders of all levels, while others provide lessons and training for beginners.

Contact: Phone: +46 70 317 30 63
Address: Silverberg Södra vägen 8, 795 96 Boda Kyrkby, Sweden
Website: https://www.silverhillstable.se/

As with any outdoor activity, it's essential to prioritize safety, respect the environment, and adhere to local rules and regulations. Additionally, it's advisable to check the weather conditions, prepare appropriate clothing and equipment, and inform someone about your planned activities and expected return time.

Indulging in Swedish Cuisine and Culinary Delights

Sweden offers a diverse range of culinary delights that combine traditional Nordic flavours with modern influences.

Looking to indulge in Swedish cuisine, here are some dishes and experiences you should explore:

Swedish Meatballs (Köttbullar):

Known worldwide, Swedish meatballs are a must-try. These flavorful meatballs are typically made from a mixture of ground beef and pork, seasoned with spices like allspice and nutmeg. They are usually served with lingonberry sauce, creamy gravy, and potatoes.

Location: Swedish Meatballs (Köttbullar): You can find delicious Swedish meatballs at Meatballs for the People in Stockholm. It's located at Nytorgsgatan 30, Södermalm. You can take the metro to Medborgarplatsen station and then walk for about 10 minutes to reach the restaurant.

Phone: + 46 8 466 60 99
Address: Nytorgsgatan 30, 116 40 Stockholm, Sweden
Website: http://meatball.se/
Smörgåsbord:

A traditional Swedish buffet, the smörgåsbord is a feast of various cold and warm dishes. It includes pickled herring, cured salmon, marinated vegetables, cold cuts, cheeses, and crisp bread. You can find smörgåsbord spreads at many restaurants, especially during festive occasions.

Location: Visit the renowned restaurant, Tradition, located at Drottninggatan 47 in Stockholm. It offers an authentic smörgåsbord experience. You can reach the restaurant by taking the metro to Hötorget station and then walking for a few minutes.

Contact: Phone: +46 8 545 126 00

Address: Sandhamnsgatan 63, 115 28 Stockholm, Sweden
Website: http://www.smorgasbord.com/
Gravlax:

Location: Visit Lisa Elmqvist in Östermalm's Saluhall, located at Östermalmstorg 114 39, Stockholm. Östermalmstorg is a well-known square, easily accessible by public transportation.

Another popular dish, gravlax is cured salmon, often served as an appetizer. The salmon is traditionally seasoned with salt, sugar, and dill, and then left to marinate for a few days. It is thinly sliced and usually accompanied by a mustard sauce, dill potatoes, and bread.

Contact: Phone: +46 8 21 99 21

Toast Skagen:

This open-faced shrimp sandwich is a classic Swedish dish. It consists of a slice of bread topped with a creamy mixture of shrimp, mayonnaise, dill, and lemon juice, and sometimes garnished with fish roe. It's a delicious and refreshing option for seafood lovers.

Location: Head to Kungshallen, a food hall in Stockholm located at Kungsgatan 44. Within Kungshallen, you'll find several restaurants serving Toast Skagen. You can reach Kungshallen by taking the metro to T-Centralen station and then walking for a short distance.

Raggmunk:

Raggmunk is a traditional Swedish potato pancake. Grated potatoes are mixed with flour, milk, and eggs, then pan-fried until golden and crispy. It's often served with lingonberries and fried pork or bacon.

Location: Pay a visit to Pelikan, a historic restaurant located at Blekingegatan 40, Södermalm, Stockholm. You can reach Pelikan by taking the metro to Medborgarplatsen station and then walking for about 10 minutes.

Cinnamon Buns (Kanelbullar):

Swedes have a love affair with cinnamon buns. These sweet and aromatic pastries are made with yeast dough, rolled with a cinnamon-sugar filling, and topped with pearl sugar. They are best enjoyed with a cup of coffee.

Location: Cinnamon Buns (Kanelbullar): Check out Vete-Katten, a traditional bakery and café located at Kungsgatan 55 in Stockholm. It's situated close to T-Centralen station, making it easily accessible.

Princess Cake (Prinsesstårta):

A beloved Swedish dessert, the princess cake is a green dome-shaped cake with layers of sponge cake, raspberry jam, vanilla custard, and whipped cream. It's covered in green marzipan and often adorned with a marzipan rose.

Location: Visit Wienercaféet, a popular café located at Norrlandsgatan 44 in Stockholm. It's situated near T-Centralen station, making it convenient to reach.

Fika:

Swedish coffee culture is incomplete without fika. Join the locals in cosy cafés, enjoy a cup of coffee, and savour delicious pastries like cinnamon buns or cardamom buns.

Location: Stockholm offers numerous cosy cafés for fika. One recommendation is Café Pascal, located at Norrtullsgatan 4. It's a short walk from Odenplan metro station.

Raggmunk:

Traditional potato pancakes are made with grated potatoes, flour, milk, and eggs. Crispy on the outside and soft on the inside, they are usually served with lingonberries and fried pork or bacon.

Location: Visit Kvarnen, a historic beer hall and restaurant located at Tjärhovsgatan 4 in Stockholm. It's a short walk from the Medborgarplatsen metro station.

Smörgåstårta:

A savoury sandwich cake that resembles a layered cake. It consists of layers of bread filled with various ingredients like mayonnaise, seafood, cold cuts, and vegetables. It's a unique and impressive dish often served on special occasions.

Location: Enjoy a tasty smörgåstårta at Grillska Huset, located at Stortorget 3 in Stockholm's Old Town (Gamla Stan). You can reach it by taking the metro to Gamla Stan station and then walking for a short distance.

Kamloops:

A traditional Swedish beef stew, usually made with slow-cooked beef, onions, carrots, and spices like allspice and bay leaves. It's hearty, flavorful, and often served with boiled potatoes or mashed potatoes.

Location: Visit Pelikan, a historic restaurant located at Blekingegatan 40 in Stockholm. Pelikan is known for its traditional Swedish dishes, including kalops. To get there, you can take the metro to Medborgarplatsen station, and from there, it's just a short walk to the restaurant.

Pelikan is situated in the Södermalm neighbourhood, which is known for its vibrant atmosphere and culinary scene. The restaurant itself has a charming interior with a traditional ambience, providing a great setting to enjoy authentic Swedish cuisine.

Knäckebröd:

Crisp and thin Swedish rye bread, often eaten with butter and various toppings like cheese, cold cuts, or spreads. It's a staple in Swedish cuisine and comes in different flavours and textures.

Location: To find traditional Swedish knäckebröd, you can visit Östermalms Saluhall, a famous food market located at Östermalmstorg 114 39 in Stockholm. Several vendors within the market offer a variety of knäckebröd. You can reach Östermalms Saluhall by taking the metro to Östermalmstorg station.

Experiencing Swedish Festivals and Events

The colourful festivals and events that reflect Sweden's rich cultural past, customs, and modern art and music scene are well-known worldwide.

Here are some noteworthy Swedish festivals and events to take into consideration whether you're a traveller or tourist:

Midsummer (Midsommar):

One of Sweden's most significant holidays, Midsummer is observed on the weekend closest to the summer solstice (often around June 21). Midsommarstng is a celebration in which Swedes get together to ring in the summer by dancing around a maypole, listening to music, and eating traditional fares like pickled herring and strawberries. Outdoor activities and folk music performances are frequent features of the celebrations.

Stockholm Culture Festival:

The Stockholm Culture Festival, which takes place every August, turns the city into a thriving centre of culture. It offers a variety of activities, including musical performances, dance recitals, theatrical productions, art displays, and street performances. The event provides something for every taste and interest and is held across Stockholm in different venues.

Göteborg Film Festival:

One of Europe's premier film festivals, the Göteborg Film Festival, should be attended by movie buffs. This festival, which is held in January, features a broad range of foreign films, including debuts and retrospectives. Additionally, it provides lectures, workshops, and chances to network with people in the sector.

Way Out West:

Gothenburg hosts the well-known music event Way Out West every August. It includes a variety of foreign and Swedish musicians from different musical genres, such as rock, indie, hip-hop, and electronic music. The event provides a laid-back and ecologically sensitive ambience since it is held at Slottsskogen, a lovely park in the middle of the city.

Ice Music Festival (Jukkasjärvi):

Consider going to Jukkasjärvi's Ice Music Festival for a one-of-a-kind and memorable experience. It's in Swedish Lapland. This event features performers playing on ice instruments in a concert hall constructed completely of ice. The mood is remarkable because of the ethereal music and the enchanted winter scenery.

Lucia Celebration:

On December 13th, a customary Swedish celebration called the Lucia Celebration is conducted in honour of Saint Lucia. It entails singing traditional songs while walking among crowds of lads and girls wearing white robes. Candles, which represent the return of light after the year's darkest period, are a crucial component of the celebration. Numerous Lucia performances are held in churches and educational institutions around the nation.

Gothenburg Culture Festival:

This festival is one of the biggest cultural gatherings in Scandinavia, and it takes place in August. It has a varied schedule that includes street performances, art exhibits, theatre, dance, and music. The event takes place throughout Gothenburg, providing a wonderful chance to discover the lively cultural life of the city.

Sami Easter Festival (Jokkmokk):
In April, the Swedish Lapland town of Jokkmokk has their annual Sami Easter Festival. With traditional music, dancing, reindeer races, crafts, and gourmet delights, the event honours Sami culture. The history and way of life of the Sami people are available for visitors to learn about.

Stockholm Jazz Festival:

The October Stockholm Jazz Festival is a treat for jazz fans. Renowned worldwide and Swedish jazz players are drawn to the festival, and they play in a variety of Stockholm locations. It's a wonderful chance to get fully immersed in the city's thriving jazz culture.

Crayfish Party (Kräftskiva):

You could have the opportunity to attend a traditional Crayfish Party if you're in Sweden in August. Boiling crayfish is the main course during this celebration, which also includes singing, drinking, donning colourful paper hats, and eating. The vibrant and entertaining gathering is often conducted in parks or gardens.

Holi Festival of Colors:

The Holi Festival of Colours, which draws inspiration from the Indian holiday of Holi, is held in several Swedish towns, including Stockholm and Gothenburg. A colourful and joyful environment is created when participants assemble to throw coloured powder into the air. Live music, dancing, and vegetarian food stands are often present during the event.

Here are the specific dates, locations, and directions for the festivals and events mentioned:

Midsummer (Midsommar):

Date: Midsummer is celebrated on the weekend closest to the summer solstice, which is usually around June 21st.

Location: Midsummer celebrations take place throughout Sweden, including cities, towns, and rural areas. Popular locations for larger celebrations include Skansen (Stockholm), Drottningholm Palace (Stockholm), and Liseberg (Gothenburg).

Directions: The easiest way to get to these locations is by public transportation. You can use buses, trams, or ferries depending on the specific destination. If you prefer driving, you can rent a car and follow the road signs or use a GPS navigation system to reach your chosen location.

Stockholm Culture Festival:

Date: The Stockholm Culture Festival is held annually in August. The exact dates may vary each year

Location: The festival takes place in various locations throughout Stockholm, including parks, squares, cultural venues, and streets. Some notable venues include Kungsträdgården, Skeppsbron, and Gamla stan (Old Town).

Directions: The festival venues in Stockholm are easily accessible by public transportation, including buses, subways, and trams. Stockholm has an extensive and efficient public transportation system. If you prefer walking, many of the festival locations are within walking distance of each other, especially in the city centre.

Göteborg Film Festival:

Date: The Göteborg Film Festival is usually held in January. The specific dates may vary each year.

Location: The festival primarily takes place in Gothenburg, with screenings held in various cinemas and venues across the city, including the Draken Cinema and Göteborg Opera.

Directions: Gothenburg has an excellent public transportation system, including buses and trams. You can easily reach the festival venues by using public transport. If you prefer driving, you can rent a car and follow the road signs or use a GPS navigation system.

Way Out West:

Date: Way Out West is held annually in August. The exact dates may vary each year

Location: The festival takes place in Slottsskogen, a park located in the centre of Gothenburg.

Directions: Slottsskogen is easily accessible by public transportation in Gothenburg. You can take trams or buses to reach the park. If you prefer walking, it's feasible if you're staying in the city centre. Otherwise, public transport is a convenient option.

Ice Music Festival (Jukkasjärvi):

Date: The Ice Music Festival in Jukkasjärvi usually takes place in February.

Location: The festival is held in Jukkasjärvi, a village in Swedish Lapland. The main venue is often the Icehotel, located approximately 17 kilometres east of Kiruna.

Directions: To reach Jukkasjärvi, you can fly to Kiruna Airport and then take a taxi, shuttle bus, or rented car to the village. The Icehotel provides transportation services for festival attendees, or you can arrange your transportation. It's recommended to check the official festival website for specific transportation details and options.

Lucia Celebration:

Date: The Lucia Celebration takes place on December 13th every year.

Locations: Lucia concerts and celebrations can be found throughout Sweden, including churches, schools, and cultural venues. Many cities, such as Stockholm, Gothenburg, and Malmö, organize Lucia processions and concerts in various locations.

Directions: The venues for Lucia celebrations are typically easily accessible by public transportation, as cities in Sweden have a well-developed bus, tram, and subway networks. You can check the specific venue information for each Lucia event and plan your transportation accordingly.

Gothenburg Culture Festival:

Date: The Gothenburg Culture Festival is usually held in August.

Location: The festival takes place in various locations throughout Gothenburg, including parks, squares, streets, and cultural venues. Popular spots include Avenyn, Järntorget, and Götaplatsen.

Directions: Gothenburg has a comprehensive public transportation system, including trams and buses. Most festival venues are easily accessible by public transport. You can also explore the festival by walking, especially if you're staying in the city centre.

Sami Easter Festival (Jokkmokk):

Date: The Sami Easter Festival in Jokkmokk is held in April.

Location: The festival takes place in Jokkmokk, a small town in Swedish Lapland, approximately 800 kilometres north of Stockholm.

Directions: To reach Jokkmokk, you can fly to Luleå Airport or Kiruna Airport and then continue the journey by rental car or bus. Jokkmokk is well-connected by road, and the festival venues are usually within walking distance from the town centre.

Stockholm Jazz Festival:

Date: The Stockholm Jazz Festival is typically held in October.

Location: The festival takes place in various venues across Stockholm, including renowned jazz clubs like Fasching, Stampen, and Nalen.

Directions: Stockholm has an extensive public transportation network, including buses, subways, and trams. Most festival venues are easily accessible using public transport. Additionally, the venues are often located in or near the city centre, making them reachable on foot if you're staying in that area.

Crayfish Party (Kräftskiva):

Date: Crayfish parties are commonly held in August, particularly during the traditional crayfish season.

Locations: Crayfish parties can be found in various locations throughout Sweden, including parks, gardens, restaurants, and private homes. Many restaurants and hotels offer organized crayfish parties for visitors.

Directions: The locations of crayfish parties can vary, so it's best to check with local tourism offices, hotels, or restaurants in the area you're visiting to find out about organized parties. If attending a private crayfish party, you may need to arrange transportation or follow the host's instructions for directions.

Holi Festival of Colors:

Date: The Holi Festival of Colors is typically held during spring, usually between March and April. Dates may vary.

Locations: The festival takes place in various cities across Sweden, including Stockholm, Gothenburg, and Malmö. Check the official website for specific locations and dates.

Directions: The festival locations are typically accessible by public transportation, including buses and trains, as well as by walking. Use public transport or navigation apps to reach the specific festival venue.

When attending these festivals and events, it's always a good idea to plan your transportation. Public transportation is usually the easiest and most convenient way to reach festival locations, as parking may be limited or restricted. Additionally, follow the event organizers' guidelines and check for any special instructions or changes in transportation arrangements.

Navigating Transportation in Sweden

Navigating transportation in Sweden as a traveller or tourist can be a convenient and efficient experience. Sweden has a well-developed transportation system that includes various options such as trains, buses, trams, and ferries.

Here are some key points to consider when navigating transportation in Sweden:

Trains: Trains are an excellent way to travel between major cities and towns in Sweden. The Swedish rail network is extensive and well-connected. SJ (Swedish Railways) is the primary train operator, offering both regional and long-distance services. You can purchase tickets online or at train stations. It's advisable to book in advance, especially during peak travel seasons.

Buses: Buses are an alternative to trains, particularly for reaching smaller towns and rural areas. The bus network covers most parts of Sweden and is operated by various companies. FlixBus and Swebus are two major intercity bus operators. Tickets can be purchased online, at bus stations, or sometimes directly from the driver.

Stockholm Public Transportation: In Stockholm, the capital city, the public transportation system is extensive and efficient. It consists of buses, metro (T-bana), trams, and ferries. The SL Access card is a convenient way to pay for public transportation in Stockholm. It can be loaded with credit and used across all modes of transport. Tickets can also be purchased using mobile apps or ticket machines.

Gothenburg and Malmö Public Transportation: Similarly, Gothenburg and Malmö have well-developed public transportation systems. Västtrafik operates the buses and trams in Gothenburg, while Skånetrafiken manages the transportation network in Malmö. Both cities offer various ticket options, including single tickets, travel cards, and mobile ticketing.

Ferries: Sweden's extensive coastline and numerous islands make ferries a popular mode of transportation. Archipelagos near Stockholm, Gothenburg, and the Baltic Sea have ferry connections. Waxholmsbolaget operates the archipelago ferries in Stockholm. For longer journeys, companies like Stena Line and Viking Line provide ferry services to neighbouring countries.

Taxis: Taxis are widely available in Swedish cities and can be hailed on the street or through taxi apps. Make sure to choose licensed taxis with clearly displayed company logos and check the approximate fare before starting your journey.

Cycling: Sweden is known for its cyclist-friendly infrastructure, and many cities have well-maintained bike lanes. Bike rentals are available in major cities, allowing you to explore at your own pace.

When planning your journey, consider using online resources and apps like Google Maps, ResRobot (for train and bus schedules), and local transport authority websites for the most up-to-date information on routes, timetables, and fares.

It's worth noting that Sweden has an environmentally conscious approach, and public transportation is often preferred due to its accessibility and sustainability.

Additionally, Sweden has a high standard of road safety, and driving is generally safe and straightforward for those who prefer renting a car.

Here's a more detailed guide on navigating transportation in Sweden while staying on a budget:

Trains:

Price: Train ticket prices vary based on factors like distance and class. Booking in advance can often secure lower fares. For example, a one-way ticket from Stockholm to Gothenburg can range from 400 SEK to 800 SEK (approximately $45 to $90).

Budget tip: Look for discounted fares during off-peak hours, such as early morning or late evening. Consider using regional trains instead of high-speed options, as they tend to be more affordable. Check the SJ website or app for special promotions and discounted tickets.

Buses:

Price: Intercity bus tickets are generally cheaper than trains. For instance, a one-way ticket from Stockholm to Gothenburg can range from 200 SEK to 400 SEK (approximately $22 to $45).

Budget tip: Use budget-friendly bus operators like FlixBus or Swebus, which often offer competitive prices. Booking in advance is key to securing lower fares. Be flexible with your travel dates and consider off-peak hours for better deals.

Stockholm Public Transportation:

Price: A single-use SL Access card for Stockholm's public transportation costs around 45 SEK (approximately $5). Ticket prices vary based on zones and duration of travel.

Budget tip: Purchase a multi-day or weekly travel card if you plan to use public transportation frequently. These cards provide unlimited travel within a specific timeframe and can offer better value for money. Utilize the SL website or app to plan your journey and find the most cost-effective routes.

Gothenburg and Malmö Public Transportation:

Price: Single-use bus or tram tickets in Gothenburg and Malmö cost around 30 SEK (approximately $3.50). Travel cards for unlimited travel within a specific period are also available.

Budget tip: Opt for travel cards or passes that suit your duration of stay and travel needs. These cards often provide better value compared to buying individual tickets. Check the Västtrafik and Skånetrafiken websites or apps for ticket options and fares.

Ferries:

Price: Ferry prices vary depending on the route, distance, and operator. For example, a ferry trip from Stockholm to the Stockholm Archipelago can range from 40 SEK to 300 SEK (approximately $4.50 to $33).

Budget tip: Choose shorter ferry trips or explore nearby islands with lower fares. Waxholmsbolaget operates the archipelago ferries in Stockholm, and their website provides detailed information on routes, timetables, and prices. Research different ferry operators and compare prices to find budget-friendly options.

Taxis:

Price: Taxis in Sweden can be expensive, with starting fares of an nd 40 SEK (approximately $4.50) and additional charges per kilometre or minute.

Budget tip: Use taxis sparingly or only when necessary. Public transportation is a more budget-friendly option. If you do need a taxi, consider using ride-hailing apps like

Uber or local alternatives, as they sometimes offer lower prices or discounts.

Cycling:

Price: Bike rentals in Sweden vary based on the city and rental duration. Daily rentals can range from 100 SEK to 200 SEK (approximately $11 to $22).

Budget tip: Look for bike-sharing services in the city you're visiting, as they often provide affordable hourly or daily rates. Some hotels or accommodations may offer complimentary or discounted bike rentals, so inquire about such options. Additionally, consider exploring free or low-cost cycling routes, such as parks or dedicated cycling paths, to enjoy the scenery without any additional expenses.

Accommodation budget tips:

- Choose budget-friendly accommodations such as hostels, guesthouses, or budget hotels. These options provide basic amenities at affordable prices.
- Consider staying in shared dormitory rooms in hostels, which are usually the cheapest option for solo travellers or those on a tight budget.
- Look for deals and discounts on hotel booking websites. Many platforms offer filters to specifically search for budget accommodations.
- Consider alternative lodging options like Airbnb, where you can find affordable private rooms or entire apartments. Look for properties located slightly outside city centres for potentially lower prices.
- If you're open to it, consider Couchsurfing, a platform that connects travellers with local hosts who offer free accommodation. This not only helps you save money but also provides an opportunity to

interact with locals and gain unique insights into the destination.

Additional budget tips:

- Plan your itinerary to optimize your travel routes and minimize unnecessary transportation costs.
- Take advantage of free or low-cost attractions and activities, such as exploring parks, visiting museums on discounted or free entry days, or participating in free walking tours.
- Pack your meals or explore affordable local eateries and street food stalls to save money on dining expenses.
- Make use of local supermarkets and grocery stores to buy snacks, drinks, and essentials at lower prices compared to tourist areas.
- Consider purchasing a local SIM card or using affordable data packages to stay connected and access transportation apps or maps while on the go. This can help you navigate public transportation more efficiently and avoid unnecessary expenses.

By implementing these budget tips and being mindful of your expenses, you can explore Sweden's transportation options and enjoy your trip without breaking the bank. Remember to research and plan to find the best deals, discounts, and affordable alternatives available at your destination.

Shopping and Souvenirs in Sweden

Sweden offers a unique shopping experience for travellers and tourists, with a wide range of options to explore. From trendy fashion boutiques to traditional handicrafts.

Here are some popular shopping destinations and souvenir ideas in Sweden including transportation prices, opening hours, and highlights:

Östermalmstorg Market - Stockholm:

Location: Östermalmstorg, Stockholm.

Directions: Take the subway to Östermalmstorg station (T-bana) or use local buses to reach the market area.

Transportation prices: A single subway ticket in Stockholm costs around 40 SEK (Swedish Krona), and local bus fares start at approximately 25 SEK.

Opening hours: Östermalmstorg Market is typically open on weekdays from 9:00 AM to 6:00 PM, and Saturdays from 9:00 AM to 4:00 PM.

Highlights: At Östermalmstorg Market, you can find a delightful variety of fresh produce, local delicacies, flowers, and crafts. Look for Swedish specialities such as smoked salmon, lingonberry jam, artisanal cheeses, and traditional pastries like kanelbullar (cinnamon buns) and semlor (cardamom buns filled with almond paste and whipped cream).

Södermalm Market - Stockholm:

Location: Götgatan, Södermalm, Stockholm.

Directions: Take the subway to Slussen station (T-bana) or use local buses to reach the market area.

Transportation prices: Same as above.

Opening hours: The opening hours of shops in Södermalm Market may vary. However, most shops are open from around 10:00 AM to 6:00 PM on weekdays, with reduced hours on weekends.

Highlights: Södermalm Market is known for its vintage and second-hand shops. Explore the charming stores offering unique clothing, accessories, furniture, and collectables. You'll find a treasure trove of fashion-forward items and retro finds.

Hötorgshallen - Stockholm:

Location: Sergelgatan 29, Stockholm.

Directions: Hötorgshallen is located near T-Centralen, the central subway station in Stockholm, making it easily accessible.

Transportation prices: Same as above.

Opening hours: Hötorgshallen is open from Monday to Friday, from around 9:30 AM to 6:00 PM. On Saturdays, it is open from around 9:30 AM to 4:00 PM.

Highlights: Hötorgshallen is a bustling food market offering a wide selection of international and Swedish cuisine. Explore the stalls for fresh seafood, cheeses, meats, baked goods, and exotic spices. Treat yourself to a traditional Swedish smörgåsbord or grab a quick bite from one of the stalls.

Saluhallen Market - Gothenburg:

Location: Kungstorget, Gothenburg.

Directions: The market is centrally located, within walking distance of the main shopping areas in Gothenburg, such as Avenyn.

Transportation prices: A single tram or bus ticket in Gothenburg costs around 30 SEK.

Opening hours: Saluhallen Market is typically open on weekdays from 10:00 AM to 6:00 PM.

Highlights: Saluhallen Market offers a diverse range of fresh seafood, cheeses, meats, baked goods, and international delicacies. Indulge in local specialities like smoked prawns, pickled herring, and the famous Gothenburg shrimp sandwich.

Gamla Stan - Stockholm:

Location: Gamla Stan, Stockholm's Old Town.
Directions: Gamla Stan is easily accessible by walking or taking the subway to Gamla Stan station (T-bana). Transportation prices: Same as above.
Opening hours: Shops in Gamla Stan generally open around 10:00 AM and close around 6:00 PM. Some shops may have shorter hours on Sundays.
Highlights: Gamla Stan is famous for its narrow, cobblestone streets lined with charming shops selling souvenirs, handicrafts, and Swedish design items. Look for traditional Swedish items like Dala horses, Viking-inspired jewellery, crystal glassware, and hand-knitted woollens.

Don't miss the chance to explore the unique antique stores and art galleries scattered throughout the area.

NK (Nordiska Kompaniet) - Stockholm:

Location: Hamngatan 18-20, Stockholm.

Directions: NK is located in the heart of Stockholm, near Sergels Torg Square. It is easily accessible by walking or taking the subway to T-Centralen or Hötorget stations.

Transportation prices: Same as above.

Opening hours: NK is open on weekdays from around 10:00 AM to 7:00 PM, Saturdays from 10:00 AM to 6:00 PM, and Sundays from 11:00 AM to 6:00 PM.

Highlights: NK is a renowned department store offering a wide range of luxury brands, high-end fashion, cosmetics, and home goods. Browse through the elegant displays and explore the Swedish design section for iconic brands like Marimekko and Svenskt Tenn. NK also houses a food hall where you can find gourmet treats and delicacies.

Magasin 36 - Malmö:

Location: Södra Förstadsgatan 25, Malmö.

Directions: Magasin 36 is located in the city centre of Malmö, near the Gustav Adolfs Torg square. It is within walking distance from Malmö Central Station.

Transportation prices: Train tickets to Malmö from Stockholm can vary in price depending on the class and time of booking. On average, tickets range from 250 SEK to 600 SEK for a one-way trip.

Opening hours: Magasin 36 is open from Monday to Friday, usually from 10:00 AM to 6:00 PM. On Saturdays, the opening hours are typically from 10:00 AM to 4:00 PM.

Highlights: Magasin 36 is a trendy shopping complex that combines fashion, design, and art. Discover unique Scandinavian clothing brands, contemporary home decor, and stylish accessories. The building also houses art galleries, cafes, and restaurants, making it a vibrant cultural hub.

Understanding Swedish Society and Lifestyle

Avoid Standing Out: Blending In with Locals in Sweden

No traveller wishes to be labelled as the conspicuous tourist who inadvertently offends the locals by uttering inappropriate remarks or engaging in unacceptable behaviour. Therefore, how can visitors ensure they seamlessly merge with the Swedish community during their trip? By avoiding the following behaviours, the likelihood of a harmonious and enjoyable vacation will significantly increase.

Refrain from Discussing Finances

Under no circumstances should one inquire about individuals' incomes, the cost of their homes, or their expenses. If such information is voluntarily shared, it is best to acknowledge it with a smile and move on. It is worth noting that Sweden possesses intriguing transparency in other aspects, such as the ability to text a number and discover the earnings of anyone in the country, the value of their property, or the price they paid for those fashionable trousers from H&M.

Abstain from Saying 'Hurdy Gurdy'

Ah, the Swedish Chef from the Muppets—what a source of amusement! Doesn't his peculiar accent resemble that of the Swedes? In reality, if you were to inquire, any Swede would point out that his voice is closer to that of a deranged Norwegian. However, it is advisable not to make such inquiries, as it is not an effective way to make friends. While Swedes may politely smile at the mention of this famous Muppet character, they do not particularly find him amusing.

Avoid Marijuana Consumption

Sweden enforces strict drug laws, classifying hash as dangerous as heroin. Remarkably, the Swedish population is largely accepting of this classification. While it is not uncommon to witness Swedes indulging in excessive alcohol consumption on a Saturday night, the sight of someone lighting a joint, packing a bowl, or using a bong is exceedingly rare. Engaging in such activities is simply not part of the culture, and those who do partake tend to keep it clandestine.

Maintain a Subtle Presence

Excessive gesticulation combined with loud speech is not the Swedish way. Swedes prefer to adopt a low-key demeanour, expressing themselves in calm and measured tones while generally adhering to the renowned jäntelagen principle. However, it should be noted that this behaviour may change after a few drinks. There is a common jest in Sweden that if you encounter an exceptionally boisterous individual on the streets, they are likely to be either intoxicated, American or possibly both.

Never Objectify the Opposite Sex

Swedes have elevated the art of discreetly appreciating attractive individuals to a refined level. Learn from their example and leave catcalls or wolf whistles at home. Individuals who attempt such behaviour will not only upset the subject of their attention, potentially resulting in a reprimand, but also draw disapproval from anyone within earshot.

Avoid Religious Discussions

Less than 5% of Swedes regularly attend church services. While Sweden prides itself on its tolerance for religious diversity, this does not imply a desire to engage in religious conversations. Individuals who attempt to broach the subject will be met with painfully polite silence and tight smiles—or may find themselves caught up in a passionate debate regarding why religion should remain a personal matter, as no one wishes to be subjected to discussions of this nature.

Never Request Decaffeinated Coffee

Swedes rank among the most fervent coffee drinkers worldwide, consuming an average of 4 to 5 cups per day. The coffee they savour is known for its intense strength, aligning with their preferences. Most establishments do not even offer decaffeinated options, and if they do, it is likely to be an inferior powder diluted with water. Therefore, it is advisable to fully embrace the experience or opt for an alternative beverage.

Avoid Generalizing Swedes with Norwegians or Danes

The three Scandinavian countries, despite their shared history, hold a deep sense of pride in their distinct cultures. Among them, Sweden stands as the largest and arguably the most influential. Swedes are fiercely protective of their unique identity and are not keen on being lumped together with their Norwegian or Danish counterparts. It is crucial to appreciate and acknowledge Swedes for who they are as individuals and as a nation. Their languages, people, and even the landscapes of their country exhibit notable differences. Embracing the nuances of Swedish culture will undoubtedly foster a deeper understanding and connection with the locals.

Don't Anticipate Others Buying Rounds

In Swedish drinking culture, the expectation of someone else buying the next round is a misconception. While imbibing in bars can be relatively expensive, this practice is rooted in cultural traditions and historical factors. The regulation and control of alcohol by various authorities in the past instilled a sense of frugality among the populace. As a result, it is rare for acquaintances or strangers to buy rounds for one another. Even among close friends, this gesture may not always be the norm. If someone does offer to buy a round, they will often request the recipients to promptly reimburse them by utilizing a mobile payment method known as "swish."

By consciously avoiding these behaviours, travellers can immerse themselves in the Swedish culture more seamlessly, forging genuine connections with the locals and ensuring a smoother and more enjoyable experience throughout their holiday.

Insider Tips and Recommendations

Weather and Seasons:
- Sweden experiences four distinct seasons: spring (March to May), summer (June to August), autumn (September to November), and winter (December to February).
- Summers are relatively warm with long daylight hours, while winters can be extremely cold and dark, especially in the northern regions.
- Pack appropriate clothing and accessories according to the season you plan to visit.

Transportation:
- Public transportation is efficient and reliable in Sweden. Consider getting an "SL Access Card" for travel within Stockholm, which can be used on buses, trams, trains, and ferries.
- Trains are a popular mode of transportation for intercity travel. Check the SJ website for schedules and tickets.
- If you're visiting multiple destinations, consider purchasing the "Swedish Rail Pass" for unlimited train travel within a specific time frame.

Language:
- Swedish is the official language, but most Swedes speak English fluently. However, learning a few

basic Swedish phrases can enhance your interactions with locals and show appreciation for their culture.

Currency:

- The currency in Sweden is the Swedish Krona (SEK). Credit cards are widely accepted, but it's advisable to carry some cash for small purchases in rural areas or at local markets.

Accommodation:

- Sweden offers a range of accommodation options, from luxury hotels to budget-friendly hostels and cozy cabins.
- Considecosyaying at a traditional Swedish "stuga" (cabin) in rural areas for an authentic experience.

Fika Culture:

- Fika is a cherished Swedish tradition of taking a coffee break with pastries or sandwiches.
- Embrace the fika culture and indulge in this leisurely ritual at local cafés or bakeries, preferably with friends or locals.

Outdoor Activities:

- Sweden is known for its stunning landscapes and outdoor activities.
- Explore the numerous national parks, such as Abisko National Park, Sarek National Park, or Tyresta National Park, for hiking, camping, and wildlife spotting.
- Try "allemansrätt," the right of public access, which allows you to freely explore and camp in nature, as long as you respect the environment and property owners.

Archipelago Exploration:

- Sweden's archipelagos are a hidden gem, consisting of thousands of islands and islets.

- Visit the Stockholm Archipelago, Gothenburg Archipelago, or the High Coast Archipelago for picturesque landscapes, sailing, kayaking, and island hopping.

Traditional Cuisine:
- Indulge in Swedish cuisine by trying traditional dishes such as Swedish meatballs, gravlax (cured salmon), herring, lingonberry jam, and cinnamon buns.
- Visit local markets, like Östermalm Market Hall in Stockholm or Saluhall in Gothenburg, to sample local produce, delicacies, and artisanal products.

Cultural Experiences:
- Immerse yourself in Swedish culture by visiting museums like the Vasa Museum, Skansen Open-Air Museum, or ABBA Museum in Stockholm.
- Attend local festivals and celebrations like Midsummer (Midsommar), Lucia, or crayfish parties to experience traditional Swedish customs and traditions.

Sauna and Winter Activities:
- Saunas (bastu) are an essential part of Swedish culture. Experience the tradition of saunas and winter plunges in lakes or icy waters for an invigorating and authentic Swedish experience.
- Engage in winter activities like dog sledding, ice skating, skiing, or snowmob Engasledgingnter activities like dog snowmobile, ice skating, skiing, or snowmobilingsledgingr ski resorts include Åre, Sälen, and Riksgränsen.
- Experience the thrill of the Northern Lights (Aurora Borealis) in the northern parts of Sweden, especially during the winter months.

Unique Experiences:
- Visit the Icehotel in Jukkasjärvi, where you can sleep in a room made entirely of ice and snow.
- Explore the Treehotel in Harads, featuring unique treehouse accommodations with stunning designs and panoramic views.
- Take a reindeer sleigh ride with the indigenous Sámi people to learn about their culture and traditions.

Local Etiquette:
- Swedes value personal space and privacy. Avoid intrusive behavior and respect personal boundaries.
- Remove your shoebehaviourntering someone's home.
- Punctuality is highly regarded in Swedish culture, so be on time for appointments or scheduled activities.

Sustainable Travel:
- Sweden is known for its commitment to sustainability. Embrace eco-friendly practices during your visit, such as using public transportation, recycling, and respecting nature.
- Opt for organic and locally produced food and support businesses with environmentally friendly practices.

Explore Beyond Stockholm:
- While Stockholm is a must-visit city, don't miss out on exploring other parts of Sweden.
- Visit Gothenburg on the west coast for its charming canals, lively food scene, and the Liseberg amusement park.
- Head north to Kiruna to witness the phenomenon of the Midnight Sun during summer or go dog sledding in winter.

Local Events and Markets:

- Check local event calendarsledgingstivals, concerts, and markets happening during your visit.
- Visit Christmas markets, such as the one in Gamla Stan (Old Town) in Stockholm, for a festive experience with traditional food, crafts, and decorations.

Embrace Lagom:
- Lagom is a Swedish concept of balance and moderation. Embrace the mindset of living a balanced life, appreciating simplicity, and avoiding excess.

Get to Know the Locals:
- Interact with locals and engage in conversations to gain insights into Swedish culture, traditions, and hidden gems.
- Visit local bars or pubs to mingle with Swedes and experience their social scene.

Remember, exploring Sweden like a local means immersing yourself in the culture, embracing nature, and connecting with the people. Be open-minded, respectful, and ready to embrace the Swedish way of life.

Printed in Great Britain
by Amazon

24547082R00116